CONTENTS

I TRODUCTIO

So you think you know all there is to know about the biggest prize in world football? Reckon you can recall all the great players, great teams and moments of magic and controversy over the years? Contained in this book are over 1000 questions on qualifying and playing in the tournament – the World Cup finals. Kick off with the easy questions and work your way through the rounds to reach the tough to tackle questions at the end. We hope you enjoy attempting the questions as much as we enjoyed researching and compiling them.

About the author

Clive Gifford is an award-winning author of over eighty books including *The Kingfisher Football Encyclopedia, Football Skills and Fantastic Football*. He is the author of Hodder Children's Books' *So You Think You Know* series of quiz books including titles on *Premier League Football* and *Test Match Cricket*. Clive is a keen QPR supporter and can be contacted at his website: www.clivegifford.co.uk.

EASY QUESTIONS

QUIZ 1

1. In which country is the 2006 World Cup held? *Germany*

2. Which European team are in England's group at the 2006 World Cup? *Sewend*

3. How many times have England hosted the World Cup? *None*

4. Who managed England at the 2002 World Cup?

5. Which side won the 2002 World Cup? *Brzilla*

6. Was the smallest nation ever to win a World Cup: Italy, Uruguay, Brazil or France? *Italy*

7. England's last two 2006 qualifying matches were played at which ground? *wenbley*

8. What number shirt did the legendary Brazilian player, Pele, tend to wear? *10*

9 Which England player was sent off at the 1998 World Cup?

10 The King of Romania picked his country's team to play in the 1930 World Cup: true or false?

11 Can you unscramble the letters AAPLMRD to spell out the surname of a current England midfielder?

12 Which nation has won the World Cup the most times?

13 Who scored the infamous 'Hand of God' goal against England at the 1986 World Cup?

14 In which country was the 1994 World Cup held?

15 England striker Jermain Defoe plays club football for West Ham, Tottenham Hotspur or Birmingham City?

16 A referee at the 1962 World Cup was called Edward Charles Faultless; was he English, Scottish, Welsh or Irish?

17 Can you unscramble the letters UUUYRGA to find the winner of the very first World Cup?

18 In which year did the Women's World Cup begin: 1987, 1989 or 1991?

19 Shay Given appeared at the 2002 World Cup playing for which team?

20 What position did Italian World Cup winner Dino Zoff play?

21 Was Jules Verne, Jules Holland or Jules Rimet a pioneer in the invention of the World Cup?

22 Which England player is the son of ex-England striker, Ian Wright?

23 Can you unjumble the letters AOOLNRD to find the name of the star striker of the 2002 World Cup?

24 Which English player was sent off in the second-from-last World Cup 2006 qualifying game?

25 Kristine Lilly is a World Cup winner with which nation?

26 Who knocked England out of the 2002 World Cup?

27 Which country did Gabriel Batistuta play for?

28 Which current England player was signed by Newcastle United for £17 million?

29 France's reserve goalkeeper at the 1978 World Cup was called Dominique Dropsy: true or false?

30 Which year was the World Cup first hosted by more than one country?

31 Which England player was sent off in the 1998 World Cup?

32 Roberto Rivelino won the World Cup with which country?

33 Was Mia Hamm, Birgit Prinz or Sun Wen the leading goal scorer at the 2003 Women's World Cup?

34 For which team did England star Wayne Rooney play before transferring to Manchester United?

35 Can you unjumble the letters XIOECM to find the team that hosted the 1970 World Cup?

36 In which continent will the 2010 World Cup be held?

37 Who did England beat in the final when they won the World Cup?

38 In which country was the 1990 World Cup held?

39 Which former World Cup winner managed the Republic of Ireland in World Cups?

40 Who won the 2003 Women's World Cup?

41 Three UK nations were all in the same qualifying group for the 2006 World Cup. Can you name them?

42 Which World Cup winner was sold in 2001 for over £45 million?

43 Who did England beat 3-0 at the 2002 World Cup?

44 Who scored England's last goal of the 2006 qualifying campaign?

45 Which side did Germany beat 8-0 in the 2002 World Cup: San Marino, Jamaica or Saudi Arabia?

46 Who was in goal for England at the 2002 World Cup?

47 Which Asian side made the semi-finals of the 2002 World Cup?

48 Was the first World Cup in 1920, 1930 or 1940?

49 At the 2006 World Cup are England in Group A, B or C?

50 Were Brazil, England or Germany seeded number one for the 2006 World Cup?

1　Who won the 1998 World Cup?

2　Is the World Cup held every two, four or eight years?

3　Which was the last World Cup Final to be settled by a penalty shoot-out?

4　Michael Ballack is a star player with which 2006 World Cup side?

5　In which year did England win the World Cup?

6　Ryan Giggs has never played at a World Cup finals: true or false?

7　England's winning World Cup side included two brothers. Can you name them?

8　Was the 1958, 1962 or 1966 World Cup the first at which Pele appeared?

9　How many World Cups has England hosted?

10　For which World Cup nation does goalkeeper Edwin van der Sar play?

11 Who debuted in 2005 to become the tallest footballer ever to play for England?

12 What was hidden under a bed throughout World War II?

13 Who was captain of the England team when they won the World Cup?

14 Can you unscramble the letters, AAAONDMR to spell out the name of a former World Cup star whose two goals helped knock England out of a World Cup?

15 What are the only two countries to have won the World Cup once?

16 How many times have Uruguay won the World Cup?

17 Which country, prior to the 2006 World Cup, had the biggest gap between winning World Cups?

18 What year was the last World Cup in which no player was sent off?

19 Who hosted the World Cup in 1998?

20 Did Thierry Henry, David Trezeguet or Zinedine Zidane score two headed goals in the 1998 Final?

21 Who was England's only loss to, during their ten-game 2006 qualifying campaign?

22 For which country did the following three World Cup stars play: Rui Costa, Mario Coluna and Luis Figo?

23 Which nation has been in the Final of the last three World Cups?

24 Ex-Chelsea player Marcel Desailly played for which World Cup winning side?

25 For what country does Manchester United's Cristiano Ronaldo play?

26 Which one of these countries has reached the Final of a World Cup: Sweden, Poland or Portugal?

27 Which former Tottenham Hotspur striker is coach of the German team at the 2006 tournament?

28 Did Norway, Germany, the USA or China win the 1995 Women's World Cup?

29 Which UK team lost to Peru but beat the eventual 1978 World Cup runners-up 3-1?

30 Pele managed Brazil at two World Cups: true or false?

31 Against which team did England record their largest victory in the 2006 World Cup qualifying campaign?

32 Which African nation beat the World Cup holders in the opening game of the 2002 tournament?

33 Which USA player has scored 158 goals for her country: Brandi Chastain, Michelle Akers or Mia Hamm?

34 What was the last World Cup that England failed to qualify for?

35 Was the 1986 World Cup held in Spain, Mexico or Argentina?

36 Which Euro 2004 champions failed to qualify for the 2006 World Cup?

37 Which major European side did the Republic of Ireland beat 1-0 at the 1994 World Cup?

38 Did England play their 2002 World Cup group games in Japan or South Korea?

39 For which country did Denis Law play football?

40 Hungarian international keeper Karoly Zsak lost a finger yet played many more games for Hungary: true or false?

41 For what country does rising star Robinho play?

42 Does the Women's World Cup occur once every two, four or six years?

43 Who scored Brazil's 100th goal in World Cup finals: Pele, Zico or Rivelino?

44 Can you unscramble the letters OERNYO to spell out the name of a current England star?

45 The current World Cup trophy is made of: marble, 18-carat gold or gold-plated silver?

46 Which England goalkeeper was dropped for the last 2006 World Cup qualifying matches after a bad loss to Denmark?

47 Star striker Andrei Shevchenko plays for: the Czech Republic, Russia or the Ukraine?

48 Which South American team will be England's first opponents at the 2006 World Cup?

49 What position were England seeded for the 2006 World Cup: second, fifth or seventh?

50 Who beat Uruguay on penalties in the play-offs to reach the 2006 World Cup: Australia, Switzerland or Iran?

MEDIUM QUESTIONS

1. Will England's first game of the 2006 World Cup be in Frankfurt, Munich or Berlin?

2. Turkey won their second play-off game 4-2, but did they qualify or not for the 2006 World Cup?

3. Who knocked the Republic of Ireland out of the 2002 World Cup?

4. What nationality was World Cup pioneer, Jules Rimet?

5. At which World Cup finals did just over 300 supporters watch a game, the lowest attended match in World Cup history?

6. Which Brazilian striker was voted best player of the 1998 tournament even though he did not score the most goals?

7 In qualifying for the 2002 World Cup, which famous side did the Republic of Ireland beat 1-0 and draw with 2-2, to help knock them out?

8 How many of the seventeen World Cups have been won by South American teams?

9 Who topped the 2002 World Cup group containing the teams Portugal, USA, South Korea and Poland?

10 Who scored a hat-trick in the 1966 World Cup Final?

11 Was Gerd Muller, Gregorz Lato or Johan Cruyff the top scorer at the 1974 World Cup?

12 In which continent will the 2014 World Cup be held?

13 Gauchito was the mascot at the World Cup held in Argentina, Spain or USA?

14 Lothar Matthaus is the only outfield player to appear in five World Cups. For which country did he play?

15 What was the first name of the father of Paolo Maldini, who managed his son at the 1998 World Cup Finals?

16 Can you name either of the England midfielders who missed penalties in the 1998 shoot-out with Argentina?

17 Which 2006 World Cup nation's famous clubs include Benfica and Porto?

18 Which country has been a World Cup runner-up more often than any other side?

19 Who was the last England national team manager to play in a World Cup?

20 Was Alan Shearer, Kevin Keegan or Malcolm McDonald the last player to score five goals in a game for England?

21 Were all four goals in England's epic 1998 World Cup game versus Argentina scored in the first half, the second half or in extra time?

22 Enzo Scifo played in World Cups for: Romania, Belgium, Hungary or the Czech Republic?

23 Which side rested the 1938 World Cup's top scorer for their semi-final match and lost 2-1?

24 Including the 2002 World Cup, had Lothar Matthaus, Peter Shilton, Pele or Roberto Carlos made the most ever World Cup finals appearances?

25 Who coached the Netherlands at the 1998 World Cup: Dick Advocaat, Marco van Basten or Guus Hiddink?

26 Did the Charlton, Neville or Walter brothers both score goals in a World Cup semi-final versus Austria?

27 Which England player was sent off against Macedonia in 2002?

28 Has Ken Aston, Kim Milton Neilsen or Joel Quiniou been in charge of more World Cup matches than any other referee?

29 France hosted the World Cup for the first time in 1998: true or false?

30 Has Claudia Reyna, Tab Ramos or Cobi Jones made the most appearances for the USA men's football team?

31 Whose penalty saw England beat Argentina at the 2002 World Cup?

32 Carlos Alberto Parreira was manager of Brazil when they won the 1962, 1970 or 1994 World Cup?

33 Did France play their 2002 World Cup group games in Japan or South Korea?

34 Which Swedish 2002 World Cup goal scorer played his club football at the time for Celtic?

35 Did England play in three, five or seven games at the 2002 World Cup?

36 Which was the last World Cup finals to average more than 3.00 goals per game?

37 How many times has England reached the semi-finals of the World Cup?

38 Which World Cup hosts had to play Greece in a qualifying game to qualify for their own World Cup?

39 Which 2006 World Cup nation's clubs compete in the J-League?

40 How many of the thirteen teams at the first World Cup came from Europe: two, four, six or eight?

41 Which former Manchester United and Chelsea player played for Argentina at the 1998 World Cup?

42 Which side lost in the 1962 World Cup semi-final 5-2 but won the Third Place Play-Off 6-3?

43 Sir Stanley Matthews played in over 200, over 400 or over 700 matches without being sent off?

44 Which team topped their 2006 qualifying group ahead of Spain?

45 Did Paul Merson, Gareth Southgate or Darren Anderton take England's third penalty in the 1998 shoot-out with Argentina?

46 At the end of the 2006 qualifying campaign, how many goals for England had Frank Lampard scored?

47 Which goalkeeper was voted player of the tournament in 2002?

48 Which Midlands ground was used to host some 1966 World Cup matches?

49 How many times did Pele score four goals in a match: 7, 17, 27 or 37 times?

50 Did Luis Figo, Rui Costa or Eusebio score a hat-trick when Portugal beat North Korea 5-3 at a World Cup finals?

⚽ ⚽ **QUIZ 2** ⚽ ⚽

1 Which side beat England in a World Cup qualifier that was the last game in the old Wembley Stadium?

2   What is the record number of yellow cards given in a single World Cup game: 9, 11, 13 or 16?

3   Was the goalkeeper for Peru, Zaire or Poland nicknamed 'El Loco' for his antics, which included tackling an opposing player in the other half of the pitch at a World Cup?

4   After the 1982 World Cup, was Paolo Rossi, Dino Zoff or Franco Baresi offered free shoes for life from a company in Milan?

5   Did England, Colombia or Romania top Group G at the 1998 World Cup finals?

6   Who stepped in at the last minute to host the 2003 Women's World Cup?

7   Who was the top scorer of the 1990 World Cup?

8   Is Gabriel Batistuta's middle name Juan, Omar, Fidel or Pele?

9   The Fair Play award was first introduced by FIFA at the 1966, 1978 or 1994 World Cup?

10 Can you name either of the Scottish players who are joint top scorers for their country with 30 goals each?

11 Max Morlock was the second leading scorer at the 1954 World Cup with six goals, but which team did he play for?

12 Did Carsten Jancker, Miroslav Klose or Michael Ballack score a hat-trick for Germany when playing Saudi Arabia in the 2002 World Cup?

13 Which very famous female striker scored two goals at each of the four Women's World Cups?

14 Was the first ever penalty shoot-out at a World Cup tournament in 1982, 1986 or 1990?

15 Did Roy Keane, Paul Scholes or Alan Shearer announce his international retirement in 2005?

16 Who was managing Scotland directly before Sir Alex Ferguson?

17 Has Roberto Baggio, Claudio Gentile, Paolo Maldini or Walter Zenga made the most international appearances for Italy?

18 Which Northern Ireland player was Manchester United's leading scorer five seasons in a row but only scored nine goals for his country and never appeared at a World Cup?

19 At which World Cup was the mascot a smiling dog called Striker?

20 Did Thierry Henry, Ronaldinho, Ruud van Nistelrooy or Christian Vieri score the World Cup's 1900th goal?

21 How many times have Germany or West Germany finished second in a World Cup tournament?

22 Which two teams qualified from the 1958 World Cup group containing the teams Mexico, Sweden, Hungary and Wales?

23 Which European team was pelted with fruit and vegetables when returning home after losing to North Korea at the 1966 World Cup?

24　How many different stadiums were used for the games in the first World Cup?

25　Did Iraq, Bulgaria, South Korea or Algeria finish the 1986 World Cup with no points?

26　Who did Italy beat 4-3 in the semi-final of the 1970 World Cup?

27　Wembley Stadium was one of two London grounds used to host games in the 1966 World Cup? What was the name of the other?

28　Did Spain play their 2002 World Cup group games in Japan or South Korea?

29　CONCACAF is the organization which runs football in Oceania, Africa or North America?

30　Was the 1938 World Cup held in Italy, Brazil or France?

31　Kolo Touré and Didier Drogba play for which African nation making their World Cup debut in 2006?

32 Who knocked the USA team out of the 2002 World Cup?

33 Why were Poldi Kielholz's three goals at the World Cup notable: he wore glasses, all three were scored as a substitute, all three were penalties?

34 Did Matt Holland, Niall Quinn or Robbie Keane celebrate scoring goals at the 2002 World Cup by pretending to fire a bow and arrow?

35 Papa Bouba Diop scored three goals in the 2002 World Cup, but for which team?

36 Who did Brazil beat 4-1 in the Final of the 1970 World Cup?

37 Who was in goal for England during the 1986 World Cup?

38 At which World Cup did Paul Gascoigne start crying after being booked, meaning he would miss the potential next match?

39 Was Taylor MacDonald, Neville Southall or Lothar Matthaus the oldest footballer to play in a World Cup qualifying match?

40 Did Turkey, San Marino, Argentina or Germany score the fastest goal in international football?

41 How many games ended in penalty shoot-outs at the 2002 World Cup?

42 For which club did both Frank Lampard and his father, Frank Lampard Snr play?

43 Were eighteen members of the Zambian, Nigerian or Ethiopian national team killed in a plane crash in 1993?

44 Was Denis Law, Paul McStay or Tommy Lawton the youngest-ever footballer to play for Scotland?

45 Is Diego Maradona, Gabriel Batistuta or Hernan Crespo the leading goal scorer for Argentina?

46 Did Austria, Luxembourg or Estonia lose 32 World Cup qualifying matches in a row between 1974 and 1990?

47 When did South Africa make their first World Cup finals appearance: 1986, 1990, 1994 or 1998?

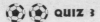

48 Which current England player bought almost an entire street of houses in Wales for his family?

49 For which of England's 2006 World Cup opponents does Dwight Yorke play?

50 Spain's second play-off game ended in a 1-1 draw. What was the score in the first match?

 QUIZ 3

1 Which team beat West Germany 8-3 but didn't win the 1954 World Cup?

2 Was Michael Owen, David Beckham or Sol Campbell the scorer of England's opening goal of the 2002 World Cup?

3 Which Italian striker was brought up in Australia where he played cricket and didn't play football competitively until he was sixteen, yet has since moved for over £20 million?

4   Ernie Brandts is the only player to have scored an own goal and a regular goal in the same match; who did he play for?

5   How many of Argentina's five penalties did they miss against England at the 1998 World Cup?

6   Which North African side has qualified for two World Cup finals, in 1982 and 1986?

7   Which England player was accused (and acquitted) of stealing jewellery at the 1970 World Cup?

8   Which World Cup winning team's players were each given a plot of land by their country's government?

9   Did Dutchman Robbie Rensenbrink score the World Cup's 500th, 750th or 1000th goal?

10 Which team won two penalty shoot-outs at the 1990 World Cup?

11 Which defending champions refused to attend the next World Cup?

12 Which England footballer was named UEFA's most valuable player for the 2004/05 Champions League season?

13 For which country has goalkeeper Antti Niemi played?

14 At which World Cup did East Germany play West Germany?

15 Did Brazil, Argentina, Ecuador or Colombia finish second in South American qualifying for the 2002 World Cup?

16 Did Jamaica, Trinidad & Tobago or Barbados make their World Cup debut in 1998?

17 Who was the first team to win the World Cup not on home soil?

18 Did Fiji, New Caledonia, the Ukraine or the Faroe Islands become the 205th and newest member of FIFA in 2004?

19 Myung-Bo Hong has made over 130 appearances for China, Thailand, South Korea or Japan?

20 Ernst Willimowski scored four goals in a 1938 World Cup game yet still ended up on the losing side. Which team did he play for?

21 If you were in Santiago watching a World Cup match, would you have been at the 1938, 1962 or 1974 World Cup?

22 Who did Uruguay beat in their final game to win the 1950 World Cup?

23 Which side has been to the most World Cups: South Korea, Denmark or Portugal?

24 Was Paul Gascoigne, Paul Parker, Paul Merson or Paul Scholes the first England player to be sent off on home soil?

24 Who was coach of Wales during their 2006 World Cup qualifying campaign?

25 Is Iain Dowie, Colin Clark or David Healy the record goal scorer for Northern Ireland?

26 Did Claudio Caniggia, Hristo Stoichkov or Roger Milla score the World Cup's 1500th goal?

28 Which great Irish goalkeeper notched up his record 119th cap for his country at the 1986 World Cup?

29 Which one of these countries has reached the semi-final of a World Cup: Ukraine, Finland or Belgium?

30 Which footballer scored his first ever penalty for England at the 2002 World Cup finals?

31 Tip and Tap were the two mascots at which World Cup?

32 Which Japanese World Cup player has played for Parma, Roma, Perugia, Bologna and in 2005, Bolton Wanderers?

33 Which small midfielder scored a spectacular goal in Scotland's 3-2 win over Holland?

34 Was Bobby Charlton, Pele or Eusebio the 1966 World Cup top scorer?

35 Which England striker scored within ten seconds of arriving as a substitute versus Greece in 2001?

36 In their qualifying group for the 2006 World Cup, can you name either team that finished above Scotland?

37 How many times has Italy hosted a World Cup?

38 Bora Milutinovic has managed two, three, four or five different countries to qualify for World Cup finals?

39 How many penalty shoot-outs have England been involved in at World Cups?

40 Juan Lopez was in charge of which team at the 1930 and the 1950 World Cup?

41 Who beat England in the group stage of the 1998 World Cup?

42 Is CONMEBOL the organization which runs football in Asia, North and Central America or South America?

43 What was the first World Cup finals to feature Cameroon: 1982, 1990 or 1994?

44 Did Brazil, Argentina, Germany or Italy win the first Fair Play award at the World Cup?

45 Chile's Roberto Rojas faked injury in a World Cup qualifying game in 1989 against which country?

46 Cesar Luis Menotti coached which team to a World Cup triumph: Argentina 1978, Italy 1982 or Argentina 1986?

47 In which year did Sven-Goran Eriksson become manager of England?

48 Which African team finished level on points in their 1982 World Cup group with the eventual champions, Italy?

49 Dennis Lawrence scored the goal that beat Bahrain and took Trinidad & Tobago to the 2006 World Cup. For which Welsh club does Lawrence play?

50 Who was Australia's goalkeeper in the play-off games versus Uruguay, who made crucial penalty shoot-out saves?

1   Who played in goal when England won the World Cup?

2   Which Spanish club does French star Zinedine Zidane play for?

3   Did Brazil play their 2002 World Cup group games in Japan or South Korea?

4   Whose final international goal secured West Germany the 1974 World Cup?

5   What is the name of the organization that runs football in Europe?

6   Who is Peru's leading scorer at World Cups: Nolberto Solano, Teofilio Cubillas or Jose Duarte?

7   Which World Cup winning goalkeeper lost almost all the sight in one eye after a car accident: Dino Zoff, Andoni Zubizaretta or Gordon Banks?

8   In what German city is the Olympiastadion, used to host 2006 World Cup matches?

9   Which Northern Irish player became the youngest to appear at a World Cup finals: Norman Whiteside, Tommy Doherty or George Best?

10 Whose World Cup shirt was sold in 2002 for £157,750?

11 Myung-Bo Hong was voted third-best player of the 2002 World Cup: true or false?

12 What was the only team to make their debut at the 1950 World Cup?

13 What was the name of Middlesbrough's former ground which hosted the North Korea v Italy 1966 World Cup game?

14 Did Sweden, the USA or Senegal knock Mexico out of the 2002 World Cup?

15 Robert Prosinecki scored for Yugoslavia in the 1990 World Cup but for which county did he play and score a goal in the 1998 tournament?

16 Did Manchester United buy Rio Ferdinand from Leeds United, West Ham United or Sheffield United?

17 How many players have scored five goals in a single game at the World Cup finals?

18 Was the 1995, 1999 or 2003 Women's World Cup decided by a penalty shoot-out?

19 At the 1998 World Cup, Ebbe Sand scored the fastest ever goal by a substitute, but which country did he play for?

20 At which World Cup did Stuart Pearce miss a penalty?

21 How many players received red cards in the 1994 World Cup: 4, 7, 11, 15?

22 Which defender played in all of England's games at the 1998 World Cup with the exception of the first match?

23 What country was the first to win two World Cups in a row?

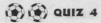

24   Which manager has managed both the
     English clubs that Michael Owen has
     played for?

25   Did the 1950, 1966 or 1998 World Cup
     feature the tournament's all-time oldest
     referee?

26   Referee Nicole Petignat officiated at: the
     1998 World Cup, the 1999 Women's
     World Cup Final or the 2002 World Cup?

27   Which English goalkeeper has kept ten
     clean sheets in World Cup finals matches?

28   Does Ledley King play for Arsenal, Aston
     Villa or Tottenham Hotspur?

29   Which South American neighbour
     thrashed Peru 6-0 at the 1978 World Cup?

30   Who is the third highest England goal
     scorer of all time: Jimmy Greaves, Michael
     Owen or Alan Shearer?

31   Prior to the 2006 World Cup, what was
     the last nation from Oceania to appear in
     a World Cup finals?

32 World Cup striker Hans Krankl played for which country?

33 Was the Goleo mascot at the 2006 World Cup designed by the workshops which brought the world Wallace and Gromit, the Muppets or the Teletubbies?

34 Did Austria, Wales or Argentina come third at the 1954 World Cup?

35 Is the current England goalkeeping coach Peter Shilton, Gordon Banks or Ray Clemence?

36 Florian Albert was joint leading goal scorer at the 1962 World Cup but did he play for France, Hungary or Czechoslovakia?

37 At which World Cup were substitutes used for the first time?

38 Which side were World Cup runners-up in 1958 but failed to qualify for the next tournament?

39 Which French World Cup-winning defender played his club football in 2004 in the Middle Eastern state of Qatar?

40 The first World Cup qualifying match played in the UK occurred in: 1937, 1949 or 1953?

41 For whom does Ronaldinho play his club football: Real Madrid, Juventus, Barcelona or Inter Milan?

42 Jose Luis Chilavert was an extrovert goalkeeper famous for scoring goals from free kicks, but for which South American country?

43 Who holds the record for the most goals scored whilst playing for England?

44 Which current England star has the middle name Mark, and was, for a short time, the youngest ever scorer at the European Championships and the Premier League?

45 When England were knocked out of the 2002 World Cup, which player scored England's goal?

46 After Germany and Brazil, which country has reached the Final of the World Cup more times than any other country?

47 Which side was knocked out of the 2002 World Cup losing 3-2 in a penalty shoot-out?

48 Which former part of the Soviet Union is making its World Cup debut as a nation in 2006?

49 Which team plays Germany in the very first game of the 2006 World Cup?

50 Was the World Cup draw made in September 2005, December 2005, January 2006 or March 2006?

QUIZ 5

1 At which World Cup was one of the teams managed by a 27 year-old coach?

2 Johan Cruyff scored in nine World Cup finals matches in a row: true or false?

3 North Korea have only reached the World Cup finals once. Was it in 1966, 1978 or 1998?

4   Did Argentina, Italy or Germany become the first team ever not to score a goal in the Final of a World Cup?

5   Which Dutch midfielder wears glasses to protect his eyes after suffering from glaucoma: Edgar Davids, Arjen Robben or Clarence Seedorf?

6   Who partnered Alan Shearer upfront when playing Argentina at the 1998 World Cup?

7   Was Marcos, Taffarel or Lucio in goal for Brazil when they won the 2002 World Cup final?

8   Is Pedro Monzon infamous as: the first player to be sent off in the Final of a World Cup, the first player to punch a referee at a World Cup or the first player to be sent off in two World Cups?

9   In 2002, did Cafu, Ronaldo, or Roberto Carlos become the first player to play in the Final of three different World Cups?

10 An Italian goalkeeper was transferred for over £32 million in 2001. Who was he?

11 Who topped The Republic of Ireland's 2006 World Cup qualifying group?

12 Is Bryan Robson, David Beckham or Gordon Banks fifth in the list of all-time England appearances, with 90 caps?

13 Matthias Sammer is one of the few players to play for two countries. Did he play more often for East Germany or the reunified Germany?

14 Which team had to beat Australia in a play-off to reach the 1966 World Cup finals: Belgium, North Korea, or Chile?

15 Which team did not turn up for a World Cup qualifying match in 1996: Estonia, Latvia or San Marino?

16 In 1982, New Zealand lost all three games in their group stage, against USSR, Brazil and Scotland. Who scored the most goals against them?

17 How many World Cups did Franz Beckenbauer appear at as either a player or manager?

18   Was Scotsman Bobby Collins responsible for scoring the World Cup's 100th, 500th or 800th goal?

19   Australian striker Damien Mori once scored a goal timed from kick-off at under four seconds, under six seconds or under ten seconds?

20   At the 1966 World Cup, which underdogs led Portugal 3-0 after only 20 minutes?

21   Pele's son played professional football; was he a striker, midfielder, defender or goalkeeper?

22   Is the record attendance for a World Cup match: 107,000, 126,000 or 199,900 spectators?

23   Have 1142 goals been scored in Men's World Cup finals, Women's World Cup qualifying games or Women's World Cup finals?

24   Turkey's Rustu Recber made more saves at the 2002 World Cup than any other keeper. Did he make: 18, 32, 40 or 51?

25 Which Italian defender played 716 times
for AC Milan and appeared at the 1990
and 1994 World Cup: Paolo Maldini,
Claudio Gentile or Franco Baresi?

26 Did American Samoa, Fiji or the Cook
Islands only score one goal but let in 34
goals in their four qualifying games for
the 2006 World Cup?

27 Did Poland, Austria or Spain top Wales's
qualifying group for the 2002 World Cup?

28 Was Mario Coluna, Eusebio or Juan Morais
captain of Portugal at the 1966 World
Cup?

29 Did Germany play their 2002 World Cup
group games in Japan or South Korea?

30 Which Italian striker served out a two-year
ban before scoring a hat-trick against
Brazil in the 1982 World Cup semi-final?

31 In the 1950s, which team beat England
6-3 at Wembley and then 7-1 in their
home country?

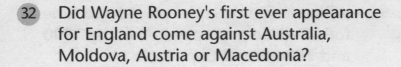

32 Did Wayne Rooney's first ever appearance for England come against Australia, Moldova, Austria or Macedonia?

33 Was Ally MacLeod, Ally McCoist or Jock Stein the manager of Scotland at the 1978 World Cup?

34 Was the first World Cup that England entered: 1930, 1950 or 1962?

35 Who was manager of the Republic of Ireland at the 1990 and 1994 World Cups?

36 Which African side at the 2006 World Cup are nicknamed 'The Elephants': Ghana, Ivory Coast, Angola or Togo?

37 Including the 2006 World Cup qualifying campaign, has David Beckham scored 11, 16, 24 or 32 goals for England?

38 Who won the first Women's World Cup?

39 In all the World Cups Portugal has reached, have they: not won, not lost or not drawn a game?

40 Which country had won the Olympics football competitions in 1924 and 1928, making them a strong case to host the first World Cup?

41 Did ex-England striker, Ian Wright, begin playing professional football at the age of 18, 20 or 22?

42 Which was the first team in the North American zone to qualify for the 2006 World Cup?

43 Which Manchester United player walked out of the Republic of Ireland team during the 2002 World Cup?

44 Rene Higuita was a goalkeeper who played for which team at the 1990 World Cup?

45 Did 14,000, 34,000, 64,000 or 84,000 spectators watch England play in a 4-4 draw at the 1954 World Cup finals?

46 Which year was the first tournament with a mascot?

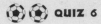

47 From what club did Frank Lampard move to Chelsea?

48 Trevor Cherry was sent off for England whilst playing Argentina, France or Germany?

49 Which European team won both of their 2006 World Cup play-off matches 1-0?

50 Which team in the 2006 World Cup's Group B were also in England's group at the 2002 tournament?

QUIZ 6

1 Who was a reserve goalkeeper to David Seaman at the 1998 World Cup finals: Tim Flowers, Chris Kirkland or David James?

2 Which German striker not only leads the World Cup finals goal scorers table but also scored a staggering 628 goals throughout his career?

3   Which one of the following was not in England's World-Cup winning side: Alan Ball, Alan Mullery or Roger Hunt?

4   In 1950, the original World Cup trophy was renamed: the Pele Cup, the Jules Rimet Cup or the Henri Delaunay Trophy?

5   Which England captain made a record 70 appearances in a row for England: David Beckham, Billy Wright or Bobby Moore?

6   Did 11, 17, 21 or 29 players receive red cards in the 2002 World Cup?

7   Which one of these countries has reached the Final of a World Cup: Yugoslavia, Hungary or the Soviet Union?

8   Who had the most shots in England's 2002 World Cup games: Michael Owen, David Beckham or Emile Heskey?

9   Has Roy Keane ever played a match in the World Cup finals?

10 Who is the oldest player ever to win the World Cup: Zinedine Zidane, Dino Zoff or Cafu?

11　Which Argentinian footballer played in four World Cups for a total of 21 appearances?

12　Which North African team did England face in their first 1998 World Cup finals game?

13　In 1958 all four UK nations reached the World Cup. Which two progressed to the quarter-finals?

14　Which Russian striker scored five goals in a single World Cup game?

15　When he scored in the World Cup Final, was Geoff Hurst playing his club football for Tottenham Hotspur, Chelsea or West Ham?

16　Against which team did Australia record the largest ever win in a World Cup qualifying game?

17　Which side managed to draw 4-4 with Brazil in the 1938 World Cup but lost in extra time?

18 The Allianz Arena – used to host 2006
World Cup finals games – is home for
which club: Schalke 04, Borussia
Dortmund or Bayern Munich?

19 Jay Jay Okocha plays football for which
African nation: Senegal, Nigeria or
Cameroon?

20 Against which team did Hakan Sükür score
the fastest ever World Cup finals goal?

21 Edson Arantes do Nascimento is better
known as which World Cup star?

22 Who was coach of Germany at the 2002
World Cup: Rudi Voller, Berti Vogts or
Jurgen Klinsmann?

23 Did Uruguay, Italy, Portugal or the Soviet
Union come third at the 1966 World Cup?

24 Did Moldova, San Marino or Albania finish
bottom of England's qualifying group for
the 2002 World Cup?

25 Was Nigeria, Togo or Ghana the first
African team to ever reach the quarter-
finals of the Women's World Cup?

26 The fastest hat-trick in international football was scored in: under four minutes, under seven minutes or under eleven minutes?

27 Jose Antonio Camacho played for and has managed which nation at World Cups?

28 Who was the Golden Boot winner for being the leading goal scorer at the 2002 World Cup?

29 Did Harry Kewell, Mark Viduka or Archie Thompson score a record thirteen goals in one of Australia's 2002 World Cup qualifying games?

30 Who did Germany beat in the Final of the 2003 Women's World Cup?

31 Who scored more goals for England: Terry Butcher, Bobby Moore or Nicky Butt?

32 To which team did England lose the Third Place Play-Off at the 1990 World Cup?

33 A referee at the 1930 World Cup was also the coach of a team there: true or false?

34   How many of their ten 2002 World Cup qualifying games did the Republic of Ireland lose?

35   Which French midfielder was voted European Footballer of the Year in 1983, 1984 and 1985?

36   How long is each period of extra time played at the World Cup if a knock-out game ends in a draw after 90 minutes?

37   Was the 1958 World Cup held in Chile, Sweden, Uruguay or Spain?

38   Against which side did Jamaica record their first ever World Cup finals win: Japan, Italy, USA or Paraguay?

39   Was Jairzinho, Gerd Muller, Zico or Paolo Rossi the last player to score in every round of a World Cup finals?

40   Stamford Bridge, Chelsea's ground, was used to host some games during the 1966 World Cup: true or false?

41   How many England players have played for their country more than 100 times?

42 Whose record did Wayne Rooney beat when he became the youngest ever England goal scorer?

43 Which Italian club did not renew Ahn Jung Hwan's contract after his goal for South Korea helped knock Italy out of the 2002 World Cup: Parma, Perugia, Fiorentina or Napoli?

44 The 1950 World Cup was hosted in which South American country?

45 In the second-from-last qualifying game for the 2006 World Cup, who took England's penalty: David Beckham, Frank Lampard or Michael Owen?

46 Sandor Kocsis was the 1954 World Cup leading goal scorer with seven, nine or eleven goals?

47 Who was 22 years and 48 days old when he became the youngest ever England captain?

48 Which Caribbean team reached the 2006 World Cup finals for the first time?

49 Was the 1990, 1994 or 1998 World Cup the first in which goalkeepers could not pick up the ball when passed back to them by a team-mate?

50 Which two teams in the 2006 World Cup's Group C played against each other in the 1978 World Cup Final?

⚽⚽ **QUIZ 7** ⚽⚽

1 Is Adriano, Carlos Lopez or Deco a striker who plays for Brazil?

2 England remained undefeated for almost a year after winning the 1966 World Cup. Who was the first to beat them: Scotland, the Netherlands, Yugoslavia or Poland?

3 Which French World Cup star became Arsenal's all-time leading goal scorer in 2005?

4 Only four countries played in all three World Cups before the Second World War. Can you name two of them?

5　Did Pele, Puskas or Eusebio score over 80 goals in international matches?

6　Which Arsenal and Dutch World Cup star has a strong fear of flying?

7　Can you name the English team who gave Peter Crouch his English league football debut?

8　Did Sam Widdowson invent corner flags, shinpads or goal nets?

9　Ronaldo's ex-wife, Milene Dominguez: is a FIFA referee; held a record for keeping a football up in the air for over nine hours; or is now married to Rivaldo?

10　Which team let in only one goal in eight games during qualifying for the 1998 World Cup yet still finished behind England in their group?

11　Was the Maracana, the Rose Bowl or the Azteca Stadium the location of the Final of two World Cups, one men's, one women's, both of which went to penalty shoot-outs?

12 Which one team beat Mexico, Argentina and Germany at the 1994 World Cup?

13 Which nation would be last in an alphabetical list of teams who have qualified for a World Cup?

14 Did Turkey, Spain or Belgium knock Japan out of the 2002 World Cup?

15 Starting with the 1962 World Cup, how many World Cup finals in a row did Bulgaria fail to win a game at?

16 French club Metz rejected a player due to frailty, who would go on to become captain of France. Was the player Laurent Blanc, Michel Platini or Zinedine Zidane?

17 Gerd Muller was the top scorer at the 1970, 1974 or 1978 World Cup?

18 Did Paolo Rossi, Roberto Baggio or Francesco Totti score five of Italy's eight goals at the 1994 World Cup?

19 Did Ruud Krol, Johnny Rep or Johann Neeskens score the first ever penalty awarded in a Final of a World Cup?

20 Was George Reader 36, 41, 44 or 53 when he refereed the 1950 World Cup Final?

21 Which striker scored 44 goals for England but only played in one World Cup finals match?

22 Germany and Brazil had never met at a World Cup tournament until the final of the 2002 World Cup: true or false?

23 Which Scandinavian side did England play in the opening game of the 2002 World Cup finals?

24 Which famous European side did North Korea beat 1-0 in their only World Cup finals appearance?

25 Prior to the 2006 tournament, how many World Cups have there been?

26 Which 2006 World Cup nation's clubs compete in the K-League?

27 At the 1982 World Cup, a prince from which country rushed on to the pitch to convince the referee to disallow a goal?

28 For which country did Franco Baresi play at World Cups?

29 Did Ronaldo, Rivaldo or Ronaldinho score a long range goal against England in the 2002 World Cup?

30 Which team at the 1930 World Cup saw their manager play in games for them?

31 Argentina made the Final of the very first World Cup. What was the next World Cup they appeared in?

32 Did Belgium, Senegal, Japan or France win the Fair Play award at the 2002 World Cup?

33 What percentage of the players at the 2002 World Cup played their club football in Europe: 40%, 60%, 75% or 85%?

34 Was Laurent Blanc, Patrick Viera or Zinedine Zidane sent off in a 1998 World Cup game, and unable to play in the Final as a result?

35 How many matches has Joel Quiniou refereed at the World Cup: 6, 8, 10, 12?

36 Did a male or female referee officiate at the 1999 Women's World Cup Final?

37 England reserve keeper, Chris Kirkland, played for which English club during the 2005/06 season?

38 Which striker suffered convulsions before the 1998 World Cup Final but played in the game?

39 What was the name of Sunderland's former ground which hosted 1966 World Cup games?

40 Can you name either of Brazil's 1970 World Cup winners who were present in the 1974 World Cup side?

41 Who won the 2004 Olympic Men's football competition?

42 Was the first player to be sent off via a referee showing a red card from Chile, Zaire, France or Romania?

43 Did South Korea, Japan or China make their debut at the 1998 World Cup finals?

44 Which famous footballer is the youngest to have scored at a World Cup?

45 Which European side let in five goals but still won a 1954 World Cup match 7-5?

46 Who won the Fair Play award at the 1982 World Cup: Argentina, Italy, Spain or Brazil?

47 From which country was the Jules Rimet trophy stolen in 1983 and never recovered?

48 Prior to the 2006 World Cup finals, how many finals matches have England played in: 20, 30, 40 or 50?

49 How many teams were seeded for the 2006 World Cup: four, eight or twelve?

50 Which European team are in Germany's group: the Czech Republic, France or Poland?

1. At the expense of which former World Cup runner-up did Scotland qualify for the 1998 World Cup?

2. Which African team went down to nine men but still managed to beat the defending champions, Argentina, at the 1990 World Cup?

3. Against which team in a 2003 friendly did Sven-Goran Eriksson make eleven substitutions?

4. The Dutch East Indies (now part of Indonesia) appeared at one World Cup finals. Can you guess which one?

5. Did Pele play almost all of his club football for Corinthians, Boca Juniors or Santos?

6. Who finished bottom of the 2002 World Cup Group A: France, Denmark, Senegal or Uruguay?

7. Canada played the first World Cup qualifying match to occur on an artificial pitch, in 1976 against which side?

8 Who finished bottom of the 1958 World Cup Group containing the teams Paraguay, France, Scotland and Yugoslavia?

9 Hristo Stoitchkov was a gifted World Cup player for Romania, Hungary or Bulgaria?

10 For which country did Paolo Rossi play World Cup football?

11 Which legendary goalkeeper was rejected by Udinese for being too small: Dino Zoff, Gianluigi Buffon or Petr Cech?

12 Swedish striker Henrik Larsson was the top scorer in the Scottish Premier League for how many seasons?

13 Can you name two of the four European teams who travelled to the very first World Cup?

14 Who won the Best Goalkeeper award at the 2002 World Cup: David Seaman, Gianluigi Buffon or Oliver Kahn?

15 Who was in charge of Scotland for 70 matches, more than any other manager of Scotland?

16 Which Portuguese World Cup player was voted FIFA World Player of the Year for 2001?

17 Ruud Krol was a World Cup star with Yugoslavia, the Netherlands, France or Belgium?

18 Which World Cup winner was also the most expensive football transfer ever?

19 How many players with the first name Alan have been sent off whilst playing for England?

20 Did England, the Republic of Ireland or France beat Romania in a penalty shoot-out at the 1990 World Cup?

21 Which member of the Brazilian eleven who started and won the 2002 World Cup Final later signed and played for Manchester United: Kleberson, Roque Junior or Roberto Carlos?

22 Which French international was signed by Arsenal for £500,000 and sold to Real Madrid for £23.5 million?

23 Sol Campbell missed the 1998 World Cup due to injury: true or false?

24 Who has played more times for their country than any other female player: Birgit Prinz, Mia Hamm, Sissi or Kristine Lilly?

25 Did Spain, Brazil or Sweden finish third at the 1950 World Cup?

26 Which England defender has played the most games for his country: Sol Campbell, Tony Adams or Kenny Sansom?

27 Italy's Alessandro Nesta is the player to be substituted the quickest in a World Cup match. After how many minutes was he replaced?

28 Was Mario Kempes, Daniel Passarella or Osvaldo Ardiles captain of the triumphant 1978 Argentinian team?

29　Which club rejected Ryan Giggs at the age of fourteen?

30　Did Johan Neeskens, Jean-Pierre Papin or Roberto Baggio score the World Cup's 1200th goal?

31　For which club did England World Cup winner Bobby Moore play almost his entire career?

32　In 1982 which side scored the most goals ever in a World Cup finals game?

33　George Best never played at a World Cup finals: true or false?

34　Which team has received seven red cards despite only appearing at five World Cups?

35　What year was the first World Cup not to be won by a team ending in the letter Y?

36　Which Scottish striker played in three World Cups in a row?

37　Gregorz Lato was top scorer at the 1958, 1978 or 1998 World Cup?

38 Which team were awarded a penalty within the first minute of a Final of a World Cup: Brazil, the Netherlands or France?

39 Who had to play Uruguay in a play-off to try to qualify for the 2006 World Cup?

40 Davor Suker was the leading goal scorer at the 1998 World Cup. How many did he score?

41 Which Russian goalkeeper was a former ice hockey goalkeeper and allegedly saved over 150 penalties in his football career?

42 Peter Shilton's last game was as captain against: Italy, France or Belgium?

43 Which Brazilian World Cup star became coach of the Japan team in 2002: Romario, Falcao or Zico?

44 Eusebio was the leading goal scorer at the 1962, 1966, 1970 or 1974 World Cup?

45 Which footballer was voted athlete of the century by the International Olympic Committee in 1999?

46 Who met South Korea in the Third Place Play-Off at the 2002 World Cup?

47 Against which major European footballing power did Michael Owen score a hat-trick in 2001?

48 Who scored England's first goal of the 1998 World Cup finals?

49 Dutchman Leo Beenhakker is the coach of which of England's World Cup opponents?

50 Is Argentina's first 2006 World Cup game against Ivory Coast, Serbia & Montenegro or Holland?

 QUIZ 9 ⚽ ⚽

1 Which legendary West German sweeper was nicknamed 'Der Kaiser'?

2 Who were the only two players with the same surname to be part of England's 1998 World Cup squad?

3   Which French defender scored the first golden goal in World Cup history?

4   Who did Scotland draw with 1-1 in their last 2006 World Cup qualifying game?

5   Zat Knight played twice for England in 2005, but for whom does he play his club football?

6   Is Diego Maradona's middle name Nelson, Armando, Sergio or Juan?

7   Which member of the England coaching team is also a manager of a Premiership club?

8   At the 1978 World Cup, who topped the group containing Spain, Brazil, Austria and Sweden?

9   Was the 1970, 1982 or 1990 World Cup the first that the Republic of Ireland managed to qualify for?

10 Was Alan Ball, Alan Mullery or Alan Shearer the first England player to be sent off in an international?

11 Who is the only English player to win the World Cup golden boot?

12 Which former Arsenal and Chelsea player scored France's third goal in the 1998 World Cup Final?

13 Against which local rivals did Pele score his first international goal?

14 How many African nations at the 2006 World Cup qualified for the first time?

15 Did David Beckham make his World Cup finals debut as a substitute against Colombia, Romania or Tunisia?

16 The Bernabeu stadium, which has hosted a World Cup Final, is found in: Mexico, Argentina, Spain or Brazil?

17 With whom does Billy Wright share the record for captaining England the most?

18 At which tournament were the most red cards awarded?

19 Who did England lose to 4-1 in a friendly match in September 2005?

20 Which Soviet goalkeeper remains the only goalkeeper to win the European Footballer of the Year award?

21 To which team did Bulgaria lose in the semi-finals of the 1994 World Cup?

22 Was Paolo Rossi, Zico or Michel Platini top scorer at the 1982 World Cup?

23 Did Gary Neville, David Beckham or Danny Mills play in every minute of England's 2002 World Cup finals?

24 Which team were beaten 9-0 by Hungary in the 1954 World Cup: Chile, Switzerland or South Korea?

25 Which Portuguese player was sold to Real Madrid from Barcelona for £37 million?

26 Up to and including the 2006 World Cup qualifying campaign, which England manager has won the most games whilst in charge: Sven-Goran Eriksson, Sir Alf Ramsey or Walter Winterbottom?

27 What nationality was the 1998 World Cup leading goal scorer, Davor Suker?

28 Against which UK side did Pele score his first World Cup goal when he was seventeen years old?

29 Did Argentina play their 2002 World Cup group games in Japan or South Korea?

30 Who is the current manager of Scotland?

31 Was the World Cup's biggest ever live attendance at Hampden Park, the San Siro or the Maracana stadium?

32 At which World Cup was the Mexican Wave first introduced?

33 Rigobert Song is the only player to have been sent off twice in World Cup finals; which team did he play for?

34 How many times has Wales qualified for the World Cup finals: once, three times or six times?

35 Was Pat Jennings, Norman Whiteside or Jimmy Nicholl playing for Toronto Blizzard at the time he appeared in the 1982 World Cup?

36 Which 1966 World Cup team's players were all in the army and had not been allowed to marry or stay up past 10 p.m. for the previous three years?

37 Against which team did Emile Heskey score in the 2002 World Cup?

38 Which team lost to the USA and Spain at the 1950 World Cup and failed to make it past the group stages?

39 How many football clubs has legendary Italian defender Paolo Maldini played for?

40 Who missed a penalty in a 1990 World Cup shoot-out: Chris Waddle, David Platt or Peter Beardsley?

41 For which country did goalkeepers Santiago Canizares and Iker Casillas play?

42 Was Pele's last international game for Brazil against Italy, England or Yugoslavia?

43 At which tournament was the mascot a smiling orange called Naranjito?

44 Larry Gaetjens is famous in World Cup history as: the first player to be sent off, the scorer of the goal that saw USA beat England 1-0 or the first referee of a World Cup final?

45 Luis Monti appeared for Argentina at the 1930 World Cup. Which European country did he play for at the next tournament?

46 Steve Sumner holds the record for most international appearances with 105 caps for which country: South Africa, Wales, New Zealand or Barbados?

47 Which team that finished in the top four of the 2002 World Cup, has England played ten times and never lost?

48 How many World Cups have been won by a team ending with the letter Y?

49 At the 2006 World Cup, are Germany in Group A, B or C?

50 How many of the eight seeded teams at the 2006 World Cup were from Europe?

1   Which 2002 World Cup winner plays for Arsenal: Rivaldo, Denilson or Gilberto Silva?

2   The first goal scored by a UK player in World Cup qualifying was by Henry Morris, but for which country?

3   Who beat Italy 2-1 in the Third Place Play-Off at the 1978 World Cup?

4   Which England player used to play for Manchester City but was signed by Chelsea in 2005?

5   Who missed the last penalty in the 1994 World Cup Final, won by Brazil?

6   Which Uruguay striker scored at the 2002 World Cup when his club at the time was Manchester United?

7   Which mountainous European country's team scored five goals in a 1954 World Cup game yet still lost the match?

8   Which keeper had more clean sheets at the 2002 World Cup than any other player: Shay Given, Brad Friedel or Oliver Kahn?

9   Carlos Alberto scored a fantastic goal in the Final of the 1970 World Cup, but in which position did he play: midfield, winger, full back or striker?

10 Chelsea player Claude Makelele plays international football for: Nigeria, France, Ghana or Cameroon?

11 Can you name one of the three players who were in the England squad at the 1950 World Cup finals and who were later knighted, taking the title 'Sir'?

12 Is the Chinese, Russian, Italian or American Women's national team nicknamed 'The Steel Roses'?

13 Did Billy Wright captain England 35, 55, 75 or 90 times?

14 Has Bryan Robson, Stuart Pearce or David Seaman played more times for England?

15 Who was voted the most entertaining team of the 2002 World Cup: Brazil, France or South Korea?

16 Juan Jose Tramutola was the youngest ever coach of a World Cup team. Was he 23, 27, 31 or 35?

17 England's Willie Hall holds the record in international football for: the fastest England goal, the first ever sending off or the fastest hat-trick?

18 Morocco drew two and won one of their 1986 group games. Did they beat Poland, Portugal or England?

19 Which famous Italian World Cup winning goalkeeper was voted 2000 World Soccer Manager of the Year?

20 Paolo Rossi was leading goal scorer at which World Cup?

21 For which English Premier League club did Hidetoshi Nakata play in the 2005/06 season?

22 At which World Cup were there four penalty shoot-outs, more than at any other World Cup?

23 Egypt first appeared at a World Cup in 1934, 1950 or 1966?

24 One of two South African players sent home from the 1998 World Cup for breaking the team's curfew was called Naughty Mokoena: true or false?

25 Who took England's first penalty in the 1998 shoot-out versus Argentina?

26 Including the 2002 World Cup, which side has scored 191 goals, far more than any other team?

27 Which team at the 1998 World Cup finals did England beat 2-0 with goals from Shearer and Scholes?

28 Italy were World Cup hosts in 1934 but did they have to qualify?

29 Has Ian Rush, Ivor Allchurch or Neville Southall played the most times for Wales?

30 Who succeeded Graham Taylor as England manager?

31   Which player, now playing in the English
     Premier League, was offside a record
     seventeen times at the 2002 World Cup,
     eight more times than any other player?

32   At which Women's World Cup were both
     the Final and the Third Place Play-Off
     decided by a penalty shoot-out?

33   Who took England's fifth penalty in the
     1998 shoot-out versus Argentina?

34   For which country did Miroslav Klose play
     at the 2002 World Cup?

35   Kharim Bagheri scored a record nineteen
     goals during qualifying for the 1998 World
     Cup, but did he play for Saudi Arabia,
     Tunisia, Senegal or Iran?

36   How many times have England played
     Germany in World Cup finals?

37   Did Gerd Muller, Paolo Rossi or Johan
     Cruyff score the World Cup finals' 700th
     goal?

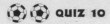

38 David Platt holds the record for the latest goal scored (after 119 minutes), but against which side?

39 At which World Cup did the USA reach the semi-finals?

40 For what club does England's Owen Hargreaves play?

41 A blind Italian boy tossed a coin to decide the fate of two teams before the 1934, 1954 or 1974 World Cup?

42 Was Martin Peters, Martin Edwards or Martin Chivers a member of the starting eleven that won England the World Cup in 1966?

43 At the 1995 Women's World Cup, did Mia Hamm, Kristine Lilley or Michelle Akers move into goal after the USA's keeper was sent off?

44 In the first two World Cups, all drawn matches were decided by penalty shoot-outs: true or false?

45 Which England striker was injured and did not play in the final games of the 1966 World Cup: Jimmy Greaves, Kevin Keegan or Roger Hunt?

46 Saeed Owairan scored the 1994 World Cup's goal of the tournament with a length-of-the-pitch run; for which country did he play?

47 Who became England's youngest ever scorer in 2003?

48 Against which European team at the 1998 World Cup did Alessandro Nesta become the player substituted the quickest?

49 Which 2006 World Cup group were Brazil placed in?

50 Can you name any of the USA's opponents in Group E?

1. What was the name of the mascot at the 1966 World Cup?

2. For which team did Kieron Dyer play before joining Newcastle United?

3. Which former World Cup player and manager of a team at the 2006 World Cup was the first non-British or Irish player to win the England Player of the Year award?

4. What position did Lev Yashin play?

5. Was Gerd Muller, Karl-Heinz Rummenige or Franz Beckenbauer captain of the West Germany side that won the 1974 World Cup?

6. How many World Cups have featured a lion as a mascot?

7. Which Argentinian is the UK's second most expensive transfer, costing £28.1 million?

8. Which gifted footballer, with the same name as an Ancient Greek scholar, captained Brazil at the 1982 and 1986 World Cups?

9   Which player's England career began in 1937 and ended in 1954, although he played his last professional club game in 1965?

10   Which UK side reached the quarter-finals of the 1982 World Cup?

11   Ernst Willimowski scored four goals in a 1938 World Cup game yet still ended up on the losing side. Which team beat his side?

12   At the 1998 World Cup, England shared the Fair Play award with which other European nation?

13   Against which British side was the fastest ever World Cup sending off?

14   Did 39, 69 or 99 nations compete in qualifying for the 2003 Women's World Cup?

15   In which country will the next Women's World Cup be?

16   Which 2006 World Cup nation includes the clubs Boca Juniors and River Plate?

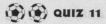

17 What is the most goals ever scored in a single World Cup finals game: eight, ten or twelve?

18 What was the first World Cup not to be held in Europe, Mexico or South America?

19 Who was the only Brazilian player to be sent off at the 2002 World Cup?

20 Around what part of the pitch did Roger Milla perform his trademark goal celebration at the 1990 World Cup?

21 To which country did Gary Lineker move to play football after his international retirement?

22 Which former World Cup-winning player managed Scotland?

23 Which Brazilian scored a hat-trick against France at the 1958 World Cup?

24 Can you name the only team to have made the semi-finals of every Women's World Cup?

25 During qualifying for the 1966 World Cup, Italy beat two countries whose names end in 'land', 6-1. Can you name the two countries?

26 Which current Chelsea player played for Argentina at the 1998 World Cup?

27 Did Niall Quinn, Robbie Keane or Matt Holland score the Republic of Ireland's equalizer during their 2002 Round of 16 game versus Spain?

28 Who managed Paul Gascoigne, Gary Lineker and the rest of the England team at the 1990 World Cup?

29 Which England goalkeeper played a record 1005 league games for a variety of clubs?

30 Rajko Mitic gashed his head on part of the stadium before starting a game and his country had to play with ten men for a while before he appeared. What was his country?

31 Which England manager played for the team in the 1950 World Cup?

32 Was Souleymane Mamam, Didier Drogba or Michael Essien the youngest ever footballer to play a World Cup qualifier?

33 Which former England international has scored more Premiership goals than any other player?

34 Was Sepp Maier, Walter Zenga or Oliver Kahn in goal for West Germany at the 1974 World Cup?

35 Which one of the following did not play for France: Just Fontaine, Raymond Kopa, Michel Platini or Kolo Touré?

36 Which World Cup was the first to feature 32 teams in the final?

37 Wilson Piazza was a World Cup-winning central defender, but for which team?

38 Who played as a defensive midfielder in England's last qualifying game for the 2006 World Cup?

39 Rio Ferdinand played in the 1998 World Cup finals for England: true or false?

40 Which European team, ranked by FIFA as the second-best side in November 2005, failed to qualify for the 2002 World Cup?

41 Which country holds the record for the biggest win in World Cup qualifying?

42 Were Chile, Paraguay or Ecuador banned from qualifying for the 1994 World Cup?

43 Was the fastest ever World Cup sending off after 56 seconds, 2 minutes 12 seconds or 3 minutes 37 seconds?

44 Which French World Cup winner was voted FIFA World Player of the Year for 2003?

45 Can you name the defender who was played in midfield by Sir Alf Ramsey and was part of the 1966 World Cup winning side?

46 Which one of these countries has reached the semi-final of the World Cup: Nigeria, Croatia or Romania?

47 Mario Kempes played 43 times for Argentina. How many red and yellow cards did he receive during those games?

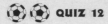

48 Who scored in both of England's last qualifying games for the 2006 World Cup?

49 How many 2006 World Cup groups contained four teams each from different continents?

50 Zlatan Ibrahimovic plays international football for which of England's opponents at the 2006 World Cup?

QUIZ 12

1 Which nation would be first in an alphabetical list of teams who have qualified for a World Cup?

2 Was Diego Simeone, Ariel Ortega or Diego Maradona the first to play for Argentina over 100 times?

3 Which Spanish side does David Beckham play for?

4 Can you name all three of Michael Owen's clubs?

5   Arsenal's ground, Highbury, was used to host some games during the 1966 World Cup: true or false?

6   Which African team are known as the Indomitable Lions and wear green shirts with red shorts?

7   Which team scored a whopping 27 goals in just five matches at the 1954 World Cup?

8   Which club did Paul Robinson play for before joining Tottenham Hotspur?

9   Does Walter Zenga, Dino Zoff or Gianluigi Buffon hold the record for the longest time between the posts without letting in a goal?

10   Which famous footballing nation has some of the world's best clubs but fourth place in the 1950 World Cup remains their highest finish?

11   The managers of which country's 1954 and 1962 World Cup teams were brothers?

12 Which England manager was an England player at the 1958 World Cup finals?

13 Which team were runners-up in both the 1974 and 1978 World Cup?

14 Who was bought for just £7500 but was top scorer in the Portuguese league in 1964, 1965, 1966, 1967, 1968, 1970 and 1973?

15 How many games ended in penalty shoot-outs at the 1998 World Cup?

16 Davor Suker made a move from which famous Spanish club to Arsenal after being top scorer at the 1998 World Cup?

17 Which Scottish player became the first to take part in four World Cups at the 1998 tournament?

18 What country was the first to win the World Cup as hosts?

19 Which European side failed to reach the 1954 World Cup finals because they lost the toss of a coin?

20 Who was manager when England last failed to qualify for a World Cup?

21 Which North American side's appearance at the 2006 World Cup is their fifth tournament in a row?

22 Maradona was the leading goal scorer at the 1986 World Cup: true or false?

23 In which South American country was the 1962 World Cup held?

24 For which English club in the 2005/06 season did Mexican striker Jared Boeghetti play?

25 FIFA's World Footballer of the Year award has run since 1991. Who is the only winner not to have appeared in a World Cup finals?

26 Against which side did one Russian striker score five goals in the 1994 World Cup?

27 To which London club did Liverpool's Steven Gerrard nearly move in the summer of 2005?

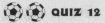
28 Who was seventeen years and 111 days old when he became the youngest ever England player?

29 Against which side did Roger Milla score to become the oldest ever World Cup goal scorer?

30 Who scored a last gasp free kick against Greece during qualifying for the 2002 World Cup?

31 Was the 1966, 1974 or 1982 World Cup the first where all the games were broadcast for television in colour?

32 Was Ernst Loertscher, Leonidas or Sandor Kocsis the first player to score an own goal at a World Cup finals?

33 Who scored just two goals in 108 appearances for England?

34 Which coach caused an outcry by not selecting Paul Gascoigne for the 1998 World Cup squad?

35 What is the only country to have scored five goals in the Final of a World Cup?

36 Which England star's middle names are Robert Joseph?

37 The Republic of Ireland finished fourth in their 2006 qualifying group. Can you name two of the three teams above them?

38 For which country does Charlton Athletic winger Dennis Rommedahl play: Croatia, the Czech Republic or Denmark?

39 Who finished his international career just one goal short of the record for the most goals by an England player?

40 The Azteca stadium, which has hosted the Final of two World Cups, is situated in which country?

41 Who did England play out a thrilling 4-4 draw with at the 1954 World Cup finals?

42 Which Scottish ex-Southampton manager played at the 1986 World Cup and was the victim of a tackle which saw the fastest ever World Cup sending off?

43 In which continent will the 2010 World Cup be held?

44 Who was England's leading scorer at the 2002 World Cup: David Beckham, Michael Owen or Sol Campbell?

45 England have won one and lost one of the World Cup penalty shoot-outs they have been involved in: true or false?

46 What country did Diego Simeone play for?

47 Which striker was substituted in favour of Michael Owen in England's second game of the 1998 World Cup?

48 Who played for England at two World Cups then managed a different side at two further World Cups?

49 Who are France's European opponents in their first game of the 2006 World Cup?

50 Who will be England's third opponents in their 2006 World Cup group?

1　Which World Cup runner-up with the Netherlands in 1974 was voted World Soccer Manager of the Year in 1987?

2　Did Italy play Hungary, Yugoslavia or Brazil in the Final of the 1938 World Cup?

3　Andres Escobar was shot dead shortly after returning to his native Colombia from the 1994 World Cup where he scored an own goal. Which team were Colombia playing?

4　At which tournament did Mario Zagallo become the first person to win a World Cup as both a player and a manager?

5　Was Rigobert Song sent off against Argentina, the Republic of Ireland or Brazil at the 1994 World Cup?

6　Is France's Lucien Laurent famous as the first player to be sent off, to score a goal or to be a substitute in the World Cup finals?

7　With which Dutch club did Johan Cruyff begin his career?

8   Luiz Felipe Scolari was the coach of which World Cup-winning team?

9   What was the first African nation to reach a World Cup quarter-finals?

10 Who was sent off whilst playing for England at the 1986 World Cup?

11 Which South American team has qualified for three World Cups yet has only played six finals matches in total?

12 Which Brazilian World Cup winner was voted FIFA World Player of the Year for 2002?

13 Which club, for a while, had Michael Owen, David Beckham, Luis Figo and Zinedine Zidane playing for them?

14 Felipe Ramos Rizo refereed three matches at the 2002 World Cup. How many red cards did he award?

15 Was the 1978, 1986 or 1994 World Cup the only time that Canada has appeared?

16 Which two Premiership players played in central defence for England in every game of the 2002 World Cup?

17 Stern John is the leading international goal scorer for Trinidad & Tobago, Jamaica or Costa Rica?

18 Did Johan Cruyff, Gerd Muller, Franz Beckenbauer or Rivelino play a game at the 1970 World Cup with a dislocated shoulder?

19 Which Asian country's team refused to play in boots and so didn't appear at the 1950 World Cup?

20 In what year did England star Frank Lampard move to Chelsea?

21 In 1981, did 120, 1200, 12,000 or 120,000 spectators watch Cameroon v Morocco in a World Cup qualifying match?

22 Can you name any one of the three countries that did not score a single point at the 2002 World Cup finals?

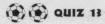
23 Did Senegal, Denmark, Brazil or Italy knock Sweden out of the 2002 World Cup?

24 Can you name the only two players for England ever to be sent off at a World Cup finals?

25 Ferenc Puskas played for two European countries at different World Cups. Can you name them both?

26 Which team appeared at the first World Cup but can no longer appear as the country has been divided into new nations?

27 At which World Cup were red and yellow cards in place for the first time?

28 Which country was coached by one man for a record 25 World Cup finals matches?

29 By how many points did England lie ahead of Poland in their 2006 World Cup qualifying group?

30 Which English striker, now a TV presenter, scored the World Cup's 1300th goal?

31 Ernst Loertscher was the first player to score a World Cup own goal, but which team did he play for?

32 Kaz, Ato and Nik were the mascots at which World Cup?

33 Which country was managed by former player Guillermo Stabile, between 1940 and 1958?

34 When Senegal met France in the 2002 World Cup, how many of France's starting eleven players played their club football in England?

35 England's quickest goal at a World Cup finals came from the boot of Kevin Keegan, Bryan Robson or Paul Gascoigne?

36 At which World Cup was the record attendance for a single game set?

37 USA goalkeeper Kasey Keller pulled a leg muscle, broke his ankle or knocked out his front teeth when pulling his golf bag out of his car in 1998?

38 Which two teams, beginning with the letter P, did South Korea beat in their 2002 World Cup group?

39 Which side have been European Champions but have only managed to qualify for one World Cup ever?

40 Who did Yugoslavia beat 9-0 at the 1974 World Cup: New Zealand, Zaire, Haiti or Chile?

41 One group at the 1950 World Cup contained only two teams, who played one game which ended 8-0. Can you name either team?

42 Did Australia beat American Samoa, Tonga or Fiji 22-0 during qualifying for the 2002 World Cup?

43 How many goals were scored against El Salvador in the biggest thrashing in World Cup finals history?

44 Against which team was the first penalty kick awarded in a Final of a World Cup: Brazil, Italy or West Germany?

45 Which Frenchman was the first footballer to be transferred for a fee in excess of £10 million: Michel Platini, Nicholas Anelka, Jean-Pierre Papin or Alain Giresse?

46 Prior to the 2006 World Cup which Italian player had made the second most appearances in the World Cup finals of any nationality?

47 Which two of the following teams played in the worst-attended World Cup finals match ever: Romania, Poland, Peru, Bulgaria?

48 Who finished bottom of the 1958 World Cup Group containing the teams West Germany, Northern Ireland, Czechoslovakia and Argentina?

49 Which European side pipped USA for the last seeded place at the 2006 World Cup?

50 Is Angola's first game at the 2006 World Cup versus Portugal, Iran or Mexico?

1 Which legendary German defender was voted World Soccer Manager of the Year in 1990?

2 Can you name two of the countries Bora Milutinovic has managed, that have reached a World Cup finals?

3 During 2006 World Cup qualifying did Scotland's Kenny Miller play club football for Bury, Wolverhampton Wanderers or Dundee?

4 Which famous footballer played for Hungary at the 1954 World Cup and for Spain at the 1962 World Cup?

5 After beating England at the 1950 World Cup, what was the next tournament the US team qualified for?

6 Was Graham Poll, Mark Halsey or Uriah Rennie the English referee at the 2002 World Cup?

7 In the African zone, which team scored the most goals but failed to qualify for the 2006 World Cup: Egypt, Algeria, Cameroon or Morocco?

8   Which was the only 2002 World Cup group to contain just one European team?

9   At the 2006 World Cup, which is the only African team to have been to a World Cup before?

10   Gordon Banks played 73 games for England. Was he on the losing side 9, 17, 21 or 33 times?

11   Which World Cup winner has been sold for transfer fees of £12.9 million, £18 million and, in 2002, £28.5 million?

12   Were most red cards awarded in the 1990, 1994 or 1998 World Cup?

13   Against which team in a 2004 friendly did Sven-Goran Eriksson make eleven substitutions: France, Mexico, Iceland or Argentina?

14   Which current England player's uncle is manager, Harry Redknapp?

15   Who captained England to a 4-0 win over Paraguay in 2002 and became the second-youngest ever England captain?

16　Which team's victory over the Czech Republic ensured that England qualified for the 2006 World Cup with one qualifying game to go?

17　Was the mother of Adriano, Robinho or Ronaldinho kidnapped in 2004 and held for 41 days?

18　What was designed by Silvio Gazzaniga, weighs 4.97kg and is valued at around £8 million?

19　In which European country is the headquarters of FIFA?

20　Sandor Kocsis is fifth in the all-time list of World Cup finals goal scorers, but how many World Cups did he take to notch up his eleven goals?

21　Who was the oldest captain ever to lift the World Cup trophy aloft: Franz Beckenbauer, Bobby Moore or Dino Zoff?

22　At which World Cup did Giuseppe Meazza's shorts fall down as he was about to take a penalty?

23 For which club did Alan Smith play before joining Manchester United?

24 Which England player was the subject of the largest ever transfer fee for a British player?

25 Which Middle Eastern nation beat the Maldives 17-0 in 1997 to break the record for the biggest win in qualifying?

26 Which player appeared in three World Cups in a row and was rejected by Liverpool at age fifteen only to be bought by them later for a record fee?

27 The new World Cup trophy has enough room on its base for winners' names up until 2014, 2022 or 2038?

28 Which one of the following teams did not qualify for the 2002 World Cup: the Netherlands, Costa Rica, Croatia or Slovenia?

29 Was the first Women's World Cup held in China, the United States or Norway?

30 Who knocked Spain out of the 2002 World Cup on penalties at the quarter-final stage: Germany, Brazil, South Korea or Turkey?

31 Who scored Romania's winner in the 1998 World Cup match against England: Dan Petrescu, Georghe Hagi or Marius Lacatus?

32 Was the first, second or third Women's World Cup the only time the hosts have won the competition?

33 Which England World Cup winner scored 199 goals for Manchester United and was knighted in 1994?

34 Did Spain make their debut at the 1930, 1934, 1938 or 1950 World Cup?

35 How old was the youngest ever footballer to play in a World Cup qualifier?

36 Did it take twelve hours, four days or two weeks for the teams from Europe to arrive in Uruguay for the very first World Cup?

37 Has David Beckham ever scored more than one goal in a game for England?

38 Liverpool's stadium, Anfield, was used to host games during the 1966 World Cup: true or false?

39 At which tournament did Roger Milla become the oldest ever World Cup goal scorer?

40 Was the first ever 0-0 draw at the 1934, 1950 or 1958 World Cup finals?

41 In which World Cup did England finish fourth?

42 Philippe Troussier has coached three teams to World Cup finals. Can you name one of them?

43 In 2003 which defender scored the second-fastest ever England goal when playing against South Africa?

44 Which major footballing power did the Republic of Ireland sensationally beat at the 1994 World Cup?

45 For which country did Mario Kempes play when he was top scorer at the 1978 World Cup?

46 What year was the first England player sent off on home soil: 1966, 1982 or 1999?

47 Who has scored more international goals: Zico, Ronaldo or Pele?

48 Which manager was shown in one British newspaper as a turnip after failing to get England to the 1994 World Cup finals?

49 Which Asian side are in Australia's group at the 2006 World Cup?

50 How many times have England met Trinidad & Tobago in a World Cup finals before?

QUIZ 15

1 Was Eric Wynalda, Brian McBride or Joe Max-Moore the first USA striker to play in three World Cups in a row?

2 Which Asian nation reached its first ever World Cup in 2002?

3 Was Santiago Canizares, David Seaman or Peter Schmeichel injured for the 2002 World Cup due to dropping a bottle of aftershave on his foot?

4 Milan Baros plays for which country: Romania, Bulgaria or the Czech Republic?

5 How many World Cup finals did Brazilian striker, Zico, appear in?

6 Despite playing for England over 70 times, Gary Neville has never scored a goal: true or false?

7 Which two teams, one Asian, one European, failed to score in three games at the 2002 World Cup?

8 Which Brazilian striker was voted most valuable player at the 1994 World Cup: Zico, Bebeto or Romario?

9 Which one of the following was a reserve goalkeeper to David Seaman at the 1998 World Cup finals: Dave Beasant, Paul Gerrard or Nigel Martyn?

10 Who coached South Korea to the semi-finals of the 2002 World Cup?

11 Is Michelle Akers, Mia Hamm or Birgit Prinz the all-time leading goal scorer at the Women's World Cups?

12 For what country did Gregorz Lato play?

13 Who was the only team England beat in their 2002 World Cup group?

14 Who had a record 21 shots on target during the 2002 World Cup: Ronaldo, Michael Ballack, Thierry Henry or Landon Donovan?

15 How many games were played in the 1990 World Cup: 32, 48, 52 or 60?

16 Bruce Arena is the coach of: Australia, Angola, or USA?

17 Did the youngest ever footballer to play in a World Cup qualifier debut for Togo, Ivory Coast or Ghana in 2001?

18 Who scored more goals for England: David Platt, Kevin Keegan or Paul Scholes?

19 Giovanni Trapattoni played for Italy at the 1962 World Cup finals but at which World Cup did he manage Italy?

20 In which year did the first World Cup become Brazil's property for ever?

21 Which UK side sensationally beat the hosts, Spain, at the 1982 World Cup?

22 Which one of these countries has reached the semi-final of the World Cup: Chile, Scotland or Colombia?

23 For which country does Liverpool defender, John Arne Riise play?

24 Was Ali Daei, Park Ji-Sung or Hidetoshi Nakata top scorer in the Asian Zone during 2006 qualifying?

25 Whose metatarsal injury kept the English nation awake in the weeks before the 2002 World Cup?

26 Which country has won more FIFA Fair Play awards at the World Cup than any other?

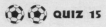

27 What was the surname of the bald Italian referee who was in charge of the 2002 Final?

28 Gerry Armstrong was the last player to score a goal for Wales, Northern Ireland or Scotland at a World Cup finals?

29 Who stepped down as the Republic of Ireland's coach after they failed to qualify for the 2006 World Cup?

30 Guillermo Stabile was the highest goal scorer at the 1930, 1950 or 1962 World Cup?

31 Which national team did Sir Alex Ferguson manage?

32 Who managed Germany at the 1998 World Cup and later managed a British national side?

33 Prior to the 2006 World Cup, which was the only World Cup that Australia had managed to qualify for?

34 Which African team caused a sensation by beating Spain at the 1998 World Cup?

35 Hakan Sükür is the scorer of the fastest ever World Cup goal. At which tournament did it occur?

36 Which was the first team in the South American zone to qualify for the 2006 tournament?

37 Who was Scotland's coach at the 1998 World Cup finals?

38 Which flamboyant goalkeeper played for France during the 1998 World Cup?

39 Which country was the first to lose the Final of a World Cup on a penalty shoot-out?

40 Scotland's most capped player is: Ally McCoist, Kenny Dalglish or Jim Leighton?

41 Where was the 1982 World Cup held?

42 At which World Cup finals were 88 goals scored in 22 games?

43 Franz Binder scored sixteen goals in nineteen games for Austria, Germany or Czechoslovakia?

44 How many years old was Wayne Rooney when he scored for England for the first time?

45 Which side finished higher in their 2006 qualifying group: Wales or Northern Ireland?

46 Which one of these countries has reached the semi-final of the World Cup: Paraguay, Japan, Republic of Ireland or Norway?

47 Has Pele, Cafu, Ronaldo or Roberto Carlos played the most ever games for Brazil?

48 Which Scandinavian side beat Cuba 8-0 in the 1938 tournament?

49 When was the last time that England met Paraguay at a World Cup finals?

50 Roque Santa Cruz plays for Bayern Munich, but for which of England's 2006 World Cup opponents does he play?

1. Was Gerd Muller, Karl-Heinz Rummenige or Franz Beckenbauer manager of the West German side that won the 1990 World Cup?

2. Have 6, 21 or 45 games in the World Cup gone to extra time?

3. Can you name the only country to have let in five goals in the Final of a World Cup?

4. Which African side at the 2006 World Cup are nicknamed 'The Hawks': Ghana, Ivory Coast or Togo?

5. No World Cup-winning team has been managed by a foreigner: true or false?

6. Manuel Rosas Sánchez of Mexico was the first player to score a penalty, an own goal or a hat-trick?

7. 1962 World Cup star Garrincha played for Chile, Sweden, Colombia or Brazil?

8. Is the name of the Lion mascot at the 2006 World Cup: Goleo, Tigre, Rexa or Franz?

9 The finals of the 2006 World Cup is contested by how many teams?

10 Which Brazilian World Cup winner was voted FIFA World Player of the Year in 2004?

11 Which of the following two sides played in the World Cup's first ever 0-0 draw: England, Scotland, Brazil, Hungary, Yugoslavia?

12 For which African nation present at the 2006 World Cup does Chelsea's Michael Essien play?

13 At which World Cup did England win the Fair Play award outright?

14 Did the Faroe Islands, Cyprus or San Marino let in 42 goals but not score one during their eight qualifying games for the 1998 World Cup?

15 Did the USA side make it to the first round, second round or quarter-finals of the 2002 World Cup?

16 Who was the manager of the Republic of Ireland team at the 2002 World Cup?

17 What was the last World Cup finals that Scotland qualified to play in?

18 Is the Azteca, Wembley or the Maracana stadium the only ground to have hosted two Finals of Men's World Cups?

19 Whose England shirt was sold at auction for £91,750: Paul Gascoigne, Geoff Hurst, Bobby Moore or Alan Shearer?

20 Did the first time both sides didn't score in the Final of a World Cup occur in 1938, 1962 or 1990?

21 How many players took part in the 2002 World Cup: 209, 274, 351 or 422?

22 Which team needed a golden goal to beat Senegal in the quarter-finals of the 2002 World Cup?

23 Is Angola, Togo or the Ivory Coast the smallest African nation to reach the World Cup?

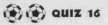

24 What nationality was the player who has scored more goals at a single World Cup than any other?

25 Enzo Bearzot won a World Cup as manager of Argentina, Uruguay or Italy?

26 Who finished the 1998 World Cup in fourth place?

27 For what South American country did Carlos Valderrama play?

28 Did Ronaldo score six, eight or eleven goals at the 2002 World Cup?

29 Which legendary German striker scored 68 goals in just 62 international appearances?

30 Which current England player was the subject of two of the top eight most expensive transfers in British football?

31 Which African nation expected to host the 2006 World Cup, but was eventually beaten by Germany?

32 Enzo Scifo appeared in how many World Cups: one, two, three or four?

33 Which side surprisingly knocked Germany out of the 1994 World Cup at the quarter-finals stage?

34 Was Rigobert Song sent off against Chile, Norway or Belgium at the 1998 World Cup?

35 Did Hakan Sükür's fastest-ever World Cup goal come after seven, eleven, fifteen or nineteen seconds?

36 Has Croatia not won, not lost or not drawn a game in all the World Cups they have reached?

37 Luke Young played in the 2006 World Cup qualifiers for England. What club was he playing for at the time?

38 Italian striker Luigi Riva once broke the arm of a spectator with one of his shots: true or false?

39 Who recorded Germany's biggest home defeat during qualifying for the 2002 World Cup?

40 Was Pele, Vava, Garrincha or Florian Albert left crippled by polio as a child, with one leg six centimetres shorter than the other?

41 Johnny Rep played for Sweden, Switzerland or the Netherlands?

42 Which South American side thrashed Scotland 7-0 at the 1954 World Cup?

43 One team has won the World Cup three times in a row: true or false?

44 Which defender played in England's first match of the 1998 World Cup but no other?

45 José Batista was the player to receive the fastest ever red card, but was he from Spain, Uruguay, Portugal or Colombia?

46 For which club did England World Cup winner Bobby Charlton play almost his entire career?

47 Which famous English football ground, where World Cup finals games have been held, cost £60,000 to build and was completed in 1910?

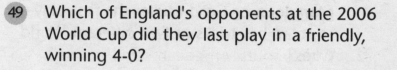

48 Iran once held the record for the biggest win in World Cup qualifying. Did their 17-0 victory come against the Maldives, Egypt or Sri Lanka?

49 Which of England's opponents at the 2006 World Cup did they last play in a friendly, winning 4-0?

50 Will South Korea's first match in the 2006 World Cup be against Togo, Switzerland or France?

QUIZ 17

1 Who was 70 years and 149 days old when he became the oldest person to manage a World Cup side: Bobby Robson, Helmut Schoen or Gaston Barreau?

2 Of the European teams at the 1998 World Cup, who scored the most points in qualifying?

3 Which team of part-time players stunned England by beating them 1-0 at the 1950 World Cup?

4   Which team, buoyed by goals from Hans Krankl, beat Sweden, Spain and West Germany at the 1978 World Cup?

5   Was Geoff Hurst, Gabriel Batistuta, Diego Maradona or Gerd Muller the first player to score hat-tricks at two different World Cups?

6   In his entire career for club and country, did Pele score 13, 27, 41 or 93 hat-tricks?

7   Which team were Olympic gold medallists in 2000 but failed to qualify for the 2006 World Cup?

8   What is the name of Germany's top club league?

9   At the 1978 World Cup, who topped the group containing Peru, Holland, Iran and Scotland?

10   Who are the only team to have been beaten by both North Korea and South Korea at World Cup finals?

11   Which member of the coaching team
      when England qualified for the 2006
      World Cup is an assistant manager at
      Bolton Wanderers?

12   At the 1966 World Cup, one team scored
      a penalty against England. Was it West
      Germany, Portugal or Mexico?

13   What was the name of the Cameroon
      striker who was a sensation at the 1990
      World Cup?

14   Peter Schmeichel appeared at World Cups
      for Denmark but can you name two of his
      three English clubs?

15   Was Vittorio Pozzo, Claudio Gentile or
      Cesare Maldini the first manager to win
      two World Cups?

16   Who were Germany playing at the 2002
      World Cup when the referee awarded a
      record number of yellow cards in a single
      World Cup game?

17   Which Danish goalkeeper started off his
      career playing as a striker?

18 Dr Leif Sward is the team doctor of which side at the 2006 World Cup?

19 Which South American side knocked England out of the 1954 World Cup?

20 Was Everton's, Manchester United's or Chelsea's stadium used to host a 1966 World Cup semi-final?

21 Which French striker scored over 180 goals in just over 300 games for his English Premier League club?

22 Was Wayne Rooney's first England goal against Moldova, Macedonia or San Marino?

23 How many games were played in the 1998 World Cup?

24 Was the 2002 World Cup final held in Kyoto, Seoul, Yokohama or Osaka?

25 Was Gerd Muller, Rudi Voller or Jurgen Klinsmann the only German player to score two hat-tricks at World Cup finals?

26 Which team at the 1998 World Cup finals did England beat 2-0 with goals from Darren Anderton and David Beckham?

27 Who was manager of England at the 1998 World Cup?

28 Which African nation has received the most red cards at World Cups?

29 Which European national team went unbeaten for over 25 matches during the mid-1990s?

30 Which team has been to more World Cups: Turkey, Tunisia or Wales?

31 At which tournament was the mascot a chilli pepper called Pique?

32 Who finished top of their qualifying zone for the 2002 World Cup: Costa Rica, USA or Mexico?

33 Which goalkeeper's first England appearance was in 1997 and his second in 2000?

34 Who won the female FIFA World Player of the Year award in both 2003 and 2004: Mia Hamm, Sun Wen or Birgit Prinz?

35 Did the Republic of Ireland play their 2002 World Cup group games in Japan or South Korea?

36 Who thrashed the eventual winners of the 1954 World Cup 8-3 in an earlier round?

37 How many nations from Asia will compete at the 2006 World Cup?

38 Who was the first country to host the World Cup twice?

39 Rinus Michels was in charge of which side at the 1974 World Cup that played an attractive style known as total football?

40 Pille is a feature at the 2006 World Cup. Is it a security robot found at each stadium, the talking ball mascot or the microchip in each match ticket?

41 Uwe Seeler holds a record with Pele for scoring in two, three or four World Cup finals?

42 Which player was known as the 'Black Pearl': Eusebio, George Weah or Leonidas?

43 At the 1994 World Cup finals, the group containing Greece also contained three teams whose name ended in the letter A. Can you name them?

44 At which World Cup was an England game interrupted by a dog running onto the pitch?

45 And who were England playing on that occasion?

46 Rene Higuita was a flamboyant goalkeeper who at the 1990 World Cup gave away a goal dribbling the ball around the pitch. Which country did he play for?

47 Only one England player was selected in FIFA's Squad of the Tournament for the 2002 World Cup. Who was it?

48 Was Lawrie Sanchez, Brian Kerr or Bryan Hamilton in charge of Northern Ireland when they recorded their historic victory over England in the 2006 qualifying campaign?

49 Which World Cup 2006 group contains both Tunisia and Saudi Arabia?

50 Which team, due to meet Brazil in the 2006 group stages, are coached by a Brazilian?

HARD QUESTIONS

1 When was the last time England beat Sweden in a competitive match?

2 Against which British team did Iran gain their first ever point at a World Cup finals?

3 Which European team qualified for 2006 letting in only one goal in their ten games?

4 How many Women's World Cups have England qualified for?

5 What was the name of the smiling cockerel which was the mascot at the 1998 World Cup?

6 Five nations bid to host the first World Cup. Can you name three of them?

7 At the first World Cup, only one non-South American nation was seeded. Who was it?

8 Of the thirteen teams at the 1999 Women's World Cup, how many were from Asia?

9 Brazil's first ever World Cup finals game ended in a 2-1 defeat to which European team?

10 Which coach received four years of free first class air travel and had a street named after him after an excellent 2002 World Cup campaign?

11 Which team scored 49 goals in sixteen 2006 World Cup qualifying games to make it to the finals?

12 Which Chelsea player came on as a substitute for his dad in an international match in 1996?

13 Against which side was the fastest goal in international football scored?

14 Who is the only player in international football to be approaching 300 international caps?

15 Who played for West Germany or Germany a total of 150 times?

16 Which team has been involved in two World Cup penalty shoot-outs and only scored one of their penalties each time?

17 Can you name any of England's three midfielders who came on as substitutes in the 1998 World Cup match versus Colombia?

18 Which European team conceded 48 goals in their 2006 World Cup qualifiers?

19 Which team scored a whopping 66 goals in their qualifying games yet still did not make the 2002 World Cup finals?

20 Before the 2002 World Cup, what was the last World Cup Turkey managed to qualify for?

21 There were 20 years between the USA's first and second World Cup finals appearance. How many years between their second and third?

22   At which World Cup finals were an average of 5.38 goals scored in each game?

23   Which South American team were originally awarded the right to host the 1986 World Cup?

24   Jorge Luis Burruchaga scored the winning goal in the Final of which World Cup?

25   Can you name either of the only two women to appear on FIFA's 100 List of all-time greatest footballers?

26   In the 1930 World Cup, the scorelines in the semi-finals were identical. The losing side scored one goal, what did the two winning sides score?

27   Which 2002 World Cup winner was released by AC Milan and played in 2004-05 for Greek side, Olympiakos?

28   Coach Hugo Meisl managed which country in 155 games?

29   Who was the referee who sent David Beckham off at the 1998 World Cup?

30 The first World Cup finals match to be played indoors was in 1994, but between which two teams?

31 Which two sides played in the first ever World Cup finals match?

32 Which two European nations took part in the first ever penalty shoot-out at a World Cup?

33 Which African nation scored the most goals in the qualifying campaign but failed to reach the 2006 finals?

34 Which team thumped Nigeria 8-0 and Canada 7-0 at the 1995 Women's World Cup?

35 Gunnar Nordahl scored 44 times in just 30 games for which country?

36 The three biggest Portuguese-speaking nations are present at the 2006 World Cup. Can you name them?

37 There was not a single draw in all the matches at which World Cup?

38   The AOL Arena is one of the stadiums of the 2006 World Cup. Which club plays their football there?

39   Which England midfielder scored four goals against San Marino in a qualifying match for the 1994 World Cup?

40   How many players tied to be the top scorer at the 1962 World Cup?

41   How many teams will contest the 2007 Women's Cup Finals?

42   Which great European player scored 83 goals in 84 international matches for one country?

43   Which former captain of a World Cup-winning side quit as manager of Uruguay in 2001?

44   In the regular 2006 qualifying campaign, not including the play-offs, who was the top scorer in the European zone?

45   Teofilio Cubillas scored ten World Cup goals, but for which country?

46 What is the most number of goals let in by a side in two consecutive games at a World Cup finals?

47 Who played for England against France in the 1966 World Cup then didn't play again for England until 1977?

48 What is the lowest ranked FIFA team to reach the 2006 World Cup finals?

49 Port Vale winger, Chris Birchall, is a member of which 2006 World Cup team?

50 Only four countries have qualified for the second round of the last three World Cups (1994, 1998, 2002). Can you name two of them?

⚽⚽⚽ **QUIZ 2** ⚽⚽⚽

1 Can you name the one defender who was in England's squads for both the 1998 and 2002 World Cups but who did not play a minute in any game?

2 Who at the 1998 tournament became the first Scotsman to appear in four World Cup finals?

3 Which two European teams have never before qualified for a World Cup?

4 Which Motown singer opened the 1994 World Cup with a failed goal attempt?

5 In the 2006 qualifying campaign, who was the top scorer in the South American zone?

6 Which team has been involved in three penalty shoot-outs at World Cups, losing them all?

7 What was the name of the dog who found the World Cup trophy which had been stolen before the 1966 tournament?

8 Which team beat Argentina 6-0 at the 2003 Women's World Cup?

9 Which two teams insisted on playing with their own football at a World Cup Final causing the referee to use a different ball for each half?

10 Who is the only player of a side competing at the 2006 World Cup, who has scored over 100 international goals?

11 How many national team managers have England had?

12 At the 1990 World Cup which team's players were promised a Rolls-Royce if they scored a goal?

13 Can you name any of the three American female players known as the 'triple-edged sword' at the 1991 Women's World Cup?

14 Who in 2001 scored against American Samoa in the twelfth minute and by the 45th minute had scored a further seven goals?

15 Which pair of brothers each have more international caps than England's leading capped player?

16 Which English referee invented red and yellow cards after witnessing a tough 1966 World Cup match?

17 Of the six European nations who had to go through play-offs for the 2006 World Cup, which had the highest FIFA World ranking?

18 Which team qualified for the 1954 World Cup as the result of a coin toss?

19 Which team, in England's group, only managed to score one goal during 2006 qualifying?

20 How many players have scored four goals in a World Cup finals game?

21 Who scored the fastest ever World Cup hat-trick?

22 Who was the only side to have won a World Cup but not qualify automatically for the 2006 World Cup?

23 Germany qualified for the 2003 Women's World Cup scoring 30 goals and letting just one in. Which side scored that goal?

24 Who was the only player to score in different World Cup finals for two different countries?

25 Which former Women's World Cup winner was coach of the USA side at the 2003 tournament?

26 Which city is the smallest (population at the time around 150,000) to have hosted the Final game of a World Cup?

27 Which goalkeeper appeared for Mexico in a record five World Cup Finals (1950, 1954, 1958, 1962 and 1966)?

28 Which former Women's World Cup player, was appointed coach of Italian men's Serie C side, Viterbese in 1999?

29 Which Caribbean nation did Bahrain have to face in a play-off for a World Cup place?

30 Who played for his American club side the day after his national team were knocked out of the 2002 World Cup?

31 Three European nations, all beginning with the letter S, had to enter the play-offs to try to qualify for the 2006 World Cup. Can you name all three of them?

32 Who is the only substitute to have ever scored a hat-trick?

33 Which team's first World Cup was 2002, when they qualified ahead of the eventual World Cup winners?

34 Can you name any of England's three midfielders who were substituted in the 1998 World Cup match versus Colombia?

35 Alphabetically, which is the first of the 2006 World Cup teams?

36 Which team topped their group at the first stage of the 1978 World Cup but didn't score a point in the second group phase?

37 How old was Mia Hamm when she made her debut for the USA team?

38 Which outfield player has played the most times for England without scoring a goal?

39 Which member of the Northern Irish 1982 World Cup side played his football at the time for the Tulsa Roughnecks?

40 Who managed Italy at one World Cup and then Paraguay at the 2002 tournament?

41 Eight of the first nine of which England player's appearances were as a substitute?

42 Which German player was sent home from the 1994 World Cup after making a rude one-fingered gesture to fans?

43 In a prison in Bangladesh, the inmates went on hunger strike when they were not allowed to watch which World Cup?

44 How old was the oldest player to appear in a World Cup qualifying match?

45 Of their first fifteen World Cup finals games, how many did England win?

46 Can you name either of the two German footballers who are the only players to have finished with their sides in first, second and third place at World Cups?

47 Who refereed a World Cup Final wearing a dinner jacket?

48 Who beat Croatia at the 2002 World Cup to record their first ever World Cup finals win?

49 Which was the only CONCACAF team to be seeded for the 2006 World Cup?

50 Who were announced as third seeds for the 2006 World Cup despite only qualifying in the play-offs?

ANSWERS

Quiz 1

1. Germany
2. Sweden
3. Once
4. Sven-Goran Eriksson
5. Brazil
6. Uruguay
7. Old Trafford
8. Number 10
9. David Beckham
10. True

11. Lampard
12. Brazil
13. Diego Maradona
14. USA
15. Tottenham Hotspur
16. Scottish
17. Uruguay
18. 1991
19. Republic of Ireland
20. Goalkeeper

21. Jules Rimet
22. Shaun Wright-Phillips
23. Ronaldo
24. David Beckham
25. USA
26. Brazil
27. Argentina
28. Michael Owen
29. True
30. 2002 (Japan and South Korea)

31. David Beckham
32. Brazil
33. Birgit Prinz

34. Everton
35. Mexico
36. Africa
37. West Germany
38. Italy
39. Jack Charlton
40. Germany

41. England, Wales, Northern Ireland
42. Zinedine Zidane
43. Denmark
44. Frank Lampard
45. Saudi Arabia
46. David Seaman
47. South Korea
48. 1930
49. Group B
50. Brazil

Quiz 2

1. France
2. Every four years
3. 1994
4. Germany
5. 1966
6. True
7. Bobby and Jackie Charlton
8. 1958
9. One
10. The Netherlands (Holland)

11. Peter Crouch
12. The World Cup trophy
13. Bobby Moore
14. Maradona
15. England and France

16. Twice
17. Italy (1938, 1982)
18. 1970
19. France
20. Zinedine Zidane

21. Northern Ireland
22. Portugal
23. Brazil
24. France
25. Portugal
26. Sweden
27. Jurgen Klinsmann
28. Norway
29. Scotland
30. False

31. Northern Ireland
32. Senegal

33. Mia Hamm
34. 1994
35. Mexico
36. Greece
37. Italy
38. Japan
39. Scotland
40. True

41. Brazil
42. Four years
43. Pele
44. Rooney
45. 18-carat gold
46. David James
47. The Ukraine
48. Paraguay
49. Second
50. Australia

MEDIUM ANSWERS

Quiz 1

1. Frankfurt
2. No
3. Spain
4. French
5. 1930 World Cup
6. Ronaldo
7. The Netherlands
8. Nine
9. South Korea
10. Geoff Hurst

11. Gregorz Lato
12. South America
13. Argentina

14. Germany/West Germany
15. Cesare Maldini
16. Paul Ince, David Batty
17. Portugal
18. Germany/West Germany
19. Glenn Hoddle
20. Malcolm McDonald

21. In the first half
22. Belgium
23. Brazil
24. Lothar Matthaus
25. Guus Hiddink
26. The Walter brothers
27. Alan Smith
28. Joel Quiniou

29. False
30. Cobi Jones

31. David Beckham
32. 1994 World Cup
33. South Korea
34. Henrik Larsson
35. Five games
36. 1958 World Cup
37. Two
38. Italy
39. Japan
40. Four

41. Juan Veron
42. France
43. Over 700 matches
44. Serbia & Montenegro
45. Paul Merson
46. Ten
47. Oliver Kahn
48. Villa Park
49. 37 times
50. Eusebio

Quiz 2

1. Germany
2. 16
3. Peru
4. Paolo Rossi
5. Romania
6. USA
7. Toto Schillachi
8. Omar
9. 1978
10. Denis Law, Kenny Dalglish

11. West Germany
12. Miroslav Klose
13. Mia Hamm

14. 1982
15. Roy Keane
16. Jock Stein
17. Paolo Maldini
18. George Best
19. USA 1994
20. Christian Vieri

21. Four
22. Wales and Sweden
23. Italy
24. Three
25. Iraq
26. West Germany
27. White City
28. South Korea
29. North America
30. France

31. Ivory Coast
32. Germany
33. He wore glasses
34. Robbie Keane
35. Senegal
36. Italy
37. Peter Shilton
38. 1990
39. Taylor MacDonald
40. San Marino

41. Two
42. West Ham
43. Zambian
44. Denis Law
45. Gabriel Batistuta
46. Luxembourg
47. 1998
48. Michael Owen
49. Trinidad & Tobago
50. 5–1

Quiz 3

1. Hungary
2. Sol Campbell
3. Christian Vieri
4. The Netherlands
5. One
6. Algeria
7. Bobby Moore
8. Uruguay
9. 1000th goal
10. Argentina

11. Uruguay
12. Steven Gerrard
13. Finland
14. 1974
15. Ecuador
16. Jamaica
17. Italy in 1938
18. New Caledonia
19. South Korea
20. Poland

21. 1962
22. Brazil
23. South Korea
24. Paul Scholes
25. Mark Hughes
26. David Healy
27. Claudio Caniggia
28. Pat Jennings
29. Belgium
30. David Beckham

31. West Germany 1974
32. Hidetoshi Nakata
33. Archie Gemmill
34. Eusebio
35. Teddy Sheringham
36. Italy, Norway
37. Twice

38. Five
39. Two
40. Uruguay

41. Romania
42. South America
43. 1982
44. Argentina
45. Brazil
46. Argentina 1978
47. 2001
48. Cameroon
49. Wrexham
50. Mark Schwarzer

Quiz 4

1. Gordon Banks
2. Real Madrid
3. South Korea
4. Gerd Muller
5. UEFA
6. Teofilio Cubillas
7. Gordon Banks
8. Berlin
9. Norman Whiteside
10. Pele

11. True
12. England
13. Ayresome Park
14. USA
15. Croatia
16. Leeds United
17. One
18. 1999 World Cup
19. Denmark
20. 1990 World Cup

21. 15
22. Gary Neville
23. Italy

24. Graeme Souness
25. The 1950 World Cup
26. The 1999 Women's World Cup Final
27. Peter Shilton
28. Tottenham Hotspur
29. Argentina
30. Jimmy Greaves

31. New Zealand (1982)
32. Austria
33. The Muppets
34. Austria
35. Ray Clemence
36. Hungary
37. 1970 World Cup
38. France
39. Marcel Desailly
40. 1949

41. Barcelona
42. Paraguay
43. Bobby Charlton
44. Wayne Rooney
45. Michael Owen
46. Italy (five times)
47. Republic of Ireland
48. Ukraine
49. Costa Rica
50. December 2005

Quiz 5

1. 1930
2. False
3. 1966
4. Argentina
5. Edgar Davids
6. Michael Owen
7. Marcos
8. The first player to be sent off in the Final of a World Cup

9. Cafu
10. Gianluigi Buffon

11. France
12. Bryan Robson
13. The reunified Germany
14. North Korea
15. Estonia
16. Scotland (five)
17. Five
18. 500th
19. Under four seconds
20. North Korea

21. Goalkeeper
22. 199,900 spectators
23. Women's World Cup qualifying games
24. 40
25. Franco Baresi
26. American Samoa
27. Poland
28. Mario Coluna
29. Japan
30. Paolo Rossi

31. Hungary
32. Australia
33. Ally MacLeod
34. 1950
35. Jackie Charlton
36. Ivory Coast
37. 16 goals
38. The United States
39. Not drawn
40. Uruguay

41. 22
42. USA
43. Roy Keane
44. Colombia.
45. 14,000

46. 1966
47. West Ham
48. Argentina
49. The Czech Republic
50. Sweden

Quiz 6

1. Tim Flowers
2. Gerd Muller
3. Alan Mullery
4. The Jules Rimet Cup
5. Billy Wright
6. 17
7. Hungary
8. David Beckham
9. No
10. Dino Zoff

11. Diego Maradona
12. Tunisia
13. Northern Ireland, Wales
14. Oleg Salenko
15. West Ham
16. American Samoa
17. Poland
18. Bayern Munich
19. Nigeria
20. South Korea

21. Pele
22. Rudi Voller
23. Portugal
24. Albania
25. Nigeria
26. Under four minutes
27. Spain
28. Ronaldo
29. Archie Thompson
30. Sweden

31. Terry Butcher (three goals)

32. Italy
33. True
34. None
35. Michel Platini
36. 15 minutes
37. Sweden
38. Japan
39. Jairzinho
40. False

41. Four
42. Michael Owen
43. Perugia
44. Brazil
45. Frank Lampard
46. Eleven goals
47. Bobby Moore
48. Trinidad and Tobago
49. The 1994 World Cup
50. Holland and Argentina

Quiz 7

1. Adriano
2. Scotland
3. Thierry Henry
4. Brazil, France, Belgium and Romania
5. Puskas
6. Dennis Bergkamp
7. Queen's Park Rangers
8. Shinpads
9. Held a record for keeping a football up in the air for over nine hours
10. Italy

11. The Rose Bowl
12. Bulgaria
13. Zaire
14. Turkey
15. Five

16. Michel Platini
17. 1970
18. Roberto Baggio
19. Johann Neeskens
20. 53 years old

21. Jimmy Greaves
22. True
23. Sweden
24. Italy
25. Seventeen
26. South Korea
27. Kuwait
28. Italy
29. Ronaldinho
30. Romania

31. 1958 World Cup
32. Belgium
33. 75%
34. Laurent Blanc
35. 8 matches
36. A female referee
37. West Bromwich Albion
38. Ronaldo
39. Roker Park
40. Jairzinho, Roberto Rivelino

41. Argentina
42. Chile
43. Japan
44. Pele
45. Austria
46. Brazil
47. Brazil
48. 50
49. Eight
50. Poland

Quiz 8

1. Sweden

2. Cameroon
3. Australia
4. 1938 World Cup
5. Santos
6. France
7. USA
8. Scotland
9. Bulgaria
10. Italy

11. Dino Zoff
12. Five
13. France, Yugoslavia, Belgium, Romania
14. Oliver Kahn
15. Craig Brown
16. Luis Figo
17. The Netherlands
18. Zinedine Zidane
19. Three (Alan Mullery, Alan Ball, Alan Smith)
20. Republic of Ireland

21. Kleberson
22. Nicholas Anelka
23. False
24. Kristine Lilly
25. Sweden
26. Kenny Sansom
27. Four
28. Daniel Passarella
29. Manchester City
30. Jean-Pierre Papin

31. West Ham United
32. Hungary
33. True
34. Cameroon
35. 1958 (the sixth tournament)
36. Kenny Dalglish
37. 1978
38. The Netherlands

39. Australia
40. Six
41. Lev Yashin
42. Italy
43. Zico
44. 1966
45. Pele
46. Turkey
47. Germany
48. Alan Shearer
49. Trinidad & Tobago
50. Ivory Coast

Quiz 9

1. Franz Beckenbauer
2. Rio Ferdinand and Les Ferdinand
3. Laurent Blanc
4. Italy
5. Fulham
6. Armando
7. Steve McClaren
8. Austria
9. The 1990 World Cup
10. Alan Mullery

11. Gary Lineker
12. Emmanuel Petit
13. Argentina
14. Four
15. Romania
16. Spain
17. Bobby Moore
18. France (22)
19. Denmark
20. Lev Yashin

21. Italy
22. Paolo Rossi
23. Danny Mills
24. South Korea

25. Luis Figo
26. Walter Winterbottom
27. Croatian
28. Wales
29. Japan
30. Walter Smith

31. The Maracana Stadium
32. Mexico 1986
33. Cameroon
34. Three times
35. Jimmy Nicholl
36. North Korea
37. Denmark
38. England
39. One (AC Milan)
40. Chris Waddle

41. Spain
42. Yugoslavia
43. Spain 1982
44. The scorer of the goal that saw USA beat England 1-0
45. Italy
46. New Zealand
47. Turkey
48. Eight
49. Group A
50. Five

Quiz 10

1. Gilberto Silva
2. Scotland
3. Brazil
4. Shaun Wright-Phillips
5. Roberto Baggio
6. Diego Forlan
7. Switzerland
8. Oliver Kahn
9. Full back
10. France

11. Sir Alf Ramsey, Sir Tom Finney, Sir Stanley Matthews
12. Chinese
13. 90 times
14. Bryan Robson
15. South Korea
16. 27
17. The fastest hat-trick
18. Portugal
19. Dino Zoff
20. 1982

21. Bolton Wanderers
22. 1990 World Cup
23. 1934
24. True
25. Alan Shearer
26. Brazil
27. David Batty
28. Yes
29. Neville Southall
30. Terry Venables

31. El Hadji Diouf
32. The 1999 Women's World Cup
33. Tunisia
34. Germany
35. Iran
36. Four
37. Gerd Muller
38. Belgium
39. 1930
40. Bayern Munich

41. 1954
42. Martin Peters
43. Mia Hamm
44. False
45. Jimmy Greaves
46. Saudi Arabia
47. Wayne Rooney
48. Austria

49. Group F
50. Ghana, Czech Republic, Italy

Quiz 11

1. World Cup Willie
2. Ipswich Town
3. Jurgen Klinsmann
4. Goalkeeper
5. Franz Beckenbauer
6. Two (England 1966 and Germany 2006)
7. Juan Sebastian Veron
8. Socrates
9. Sir Stanley Matthews
10. Northern Ireland

11. Brazil
12. France
13. Scotland
14. 99 nations
15. China
16. Argentina
17. Twelve
18. 1994 (USA)
19. Ronaldinho
20. The corner flag

21. Japan
22. Berti Vogts
23. Pele
24. USA
25. Finland, Poland
26. Hernan Crespo
27. Robbie Keane
28. Bobby Robson
29. Peter Shilton
30. Yugoslavia

31. Sir Alf Ramsey
32. Souleymane Mamam
33. Alan Shearer

34. Sepp Maier
35. Kolo Touré
36. 1998
37. Brazil (1970)
38. Ledley King
39. False
40. The Netherlands
41. Australia
42. Chile
43. 56 seconds
44. Zinedine Zidane
45. Nobby Stiles
46. Croatia
47. None
48. Frank Lampard
49. Two (Group D and Group F)
50. Sweden

Quiz 12

1. Algeria
2. Diego Simeone
3. Real Madrid
4. Liverpool, Real Madrid, Newcastle United
5. False
6. Cameroon
7. Hungary
8. Leeds United
9. Walter Zenga (517 minutes)
10. Spain

11. Brazil (Zeze and Aymore Moreira)
12. Bobby Robson
13. The Netherlands
14. Eusebio
15. Three
16. Real Madrid
17. Jim Leighton
18. Uruguay
19. Spain

20. Graham Taylor
21. USA
22. False
23. Chile
24. Bolton Wanderers
25. George Weah (Liberia)
26. Cameroon
27. Chelsea
28. Wayne Rooney
29. Russia
30. David Beckham

31. The 1974 World Cup
32. Ernst Loertscher
33. Bobby Moore
34. Glenn Hoddle
35. Brazil
36. David Beckham
37. France, Switzerland, Israel
38. Denmark
39. Gary Lineker
40. Mexico

41. Belgium
42. Gordon Strachan
43. Africa
44. Michael Owen
45. False
46. Argentina
47. Teddy Sheringham
48. Jackie Charlton
49. Switzerland
50. Sweden

Quiz 13

1. Johan Cruyff
2. Hungary
3. USA
4. 1970 World Cup
5. Brazil

6. To score a goal
7. Ajax
8. Brazil 2002
9. Cameroon
10. Ray Wilkins
11. Bolivia
12. Ronaldo
13. Real Madrid
14. Four
15. 1986
16. Sol Campbell, Rio Ferdinand
17. Trinidad & Tobago
18. Franz Beckenbauer
19. India
20. 2001

21. 120,000
22. Saudi Arabia, China, Slovenia
23. Senegal
24. David Beckham, Ray Wilkins
25. Hungary and Spain
26. Yugoslavia
27. 1970
28. West Germany
29. One
30. Gary Lineker

31. Switzerland
32. 2002
33. Argentina
34. Seven
35. Bryan Robson
36. 1950
37. Knocked out his front teeth
38. Portugal, Poland
39. Greece
40. Zaire

41. Uruguay, Bolivia
42. Tonga
43. Ten (10-1 final score)
44. West Germany

45. Jean-Pierre Papin
46. Paolo Maldini
47. Romania and Peru
48. Argentina
49. Italy
50. Portugal

Quiz 14

1. Franz Beckenbauer
2. Mexico, Costa Rica, USA, Nigeria, China, Honduras
3. Wolverhampton Wanderers
4. Ferenc Puskas
5. The 1990 World Cup
6. Graham Poll
7. Egypt
8. Group C
9. Tunisia
10. Nine times

11. Ronaldo
12. 1998 World Cup
13. Iceland
14. Frank Lampard
15. Michael Owen
16. Holland
17. Robinho
18. The current World Cup trophy
19. Switzerland
20. One

21. Dino Zoff
22. 1938 World Cup
23. Leeds United
24. Rio Ferdinand
25. Iran
26. Kenny Dalglish
27. 2038
28. The Netherlands
29. China
30. South Korea

31. Dan Petrescu
32. The third Women's World Cup
33. Bobby Charlton
34. 1934 World Cup
35. Thirteen years old
36. Two weeks
37. No
38. False
39. 1994 World Cup
40. 1958 World Cup

41. 1990 World Cup
42. Japan, Nigeria, South Africa
43. Gareth Southgate
44. Italy
45. Argentina
46. 1999
47. Pele
48. Graham Taylor
49. Japan
50. None

Quiz 15

1. Eric Wynalda
2. China
3. Santiago Canizares
4. The Czech Republic
5. Three
6. True
7. China, France
8. Romario
9. Nigel Martyn
10. Guus Hiddink

11. Michelle Akers
12. Poland
13. Argentina
14. Ronaldo
15. 52
16. USA

17. Togo
18. David Platt
19. 2002 World Cup
20. 1970

21. Northern Ireland
22. Chile
23. Norway
24. Ali Daei
25. David Beckham's
26. Brazil
27. Pierluigi Collina
28. Northern Ireland
29. Brian Kerr
30. 1930

31. Scotland
32. Berti Vogts
33. 1974
34. Nigeria
35. 2002 World Cup
36. Argentina
37. Craig Brown
38. Fabien Barthez
39. Italy
40. Kenny Dalglish

41. Spain
42. 1950 World Cup
43. Austria
44. Seventeen
45. Northern Ireland
46. Norway
47. Cafu
48. Sweden
49. The 1986 World Cup
50. Paraguay

Quiz 16

1. Franz Beckenbauer
2. 45

3. Sweden
4. Togo
5. True
6. Score a penalty
7. Brazil
8. Goleo
9. 32
10. Ronaldinho

11. Brazil and England
12. Ghana
13. 1990
14. San Marino
15. Quarter-finals
16. Mick McCarthy
17. 1998
18. Azteca Stadium
19. Geoff Hurst
20. 1990

21. 351
22. Turkey
23. Togo
24. French
25. Italy
26. The Netherlands
27. Colombia
28. Eight
29. Gerd Muller
30. Rio Ferdinand

31. South Africa
32. Four
33. Bulgaria
34. Chile
35. Eleven seconds
36. Not drawn
37. Charlton Athletic
38. True
39. England
40. Garrincha

41. The Netherlands
42. Uruguay
43. False
44. Gareth Southgate
45. Uruguay
46. Manchester United
47. Old Trafford
48. The Maldives
49. Paraguay
50. Togo

Quiz 17

1. Gaston Barreau
2. Romania
3. USA
4. Austria
5. Gabriel Batistuta
6. 93
7. Cameroon
8. The Bundesliga
9. Peru
10. Italy

11. Sammy Lee
12. Portugal
13. Roger Milla
14. Manchester United, Aston Villa,
    Manchester City
15. Vittorio Pozzo
16. Cameroon
17. Peter Schmeichel
18. England
19. Uruguay
20. Everton's

21. Thierry Henry
22. Macedonia
23. 64
24. Yokohama
25. Gerd Muller
26. Colombia

27. Glenn Hoddle
28. Cameroon
29. France
30. Tunisia

31. Mexico 1986
32. Costa Rica
33. David James
34. Birgit Prinz
35. Japan
36. Hungary
37. Four
38. Mexico

39. The Netherlands
40. The talking ball mascot

41. Four
42. Eusebio
43. Argentina, Nigeria, Bulgaria
44. The 1962 World Cup
45. Brazil
46. Colombia
47. Sol Campbell
48. Lawrie Sanchez
49. Group H
50. Japan

HARD ANSWERS

Quiz 1

1. 1968
2. Scotland
3. Serbia & Montenegro
4. One (1995)
5. Footix
6. Uruguay, Italy, Spain, Sweden and the Netherlands.
7. USA
8. Three
9. Yugoslavia
10. Guus Hiddink

11. Mexico
12. Eidur Gudjohnsen
13. England
14. Kristine Lilly
15. Lothar Matthaus
16. Mexico
17. Steve McManaman, David Batty, Robert Lee

18. Luxembourg
19. Australia
20. 1954

21. 40 years
22. 1954 World Cup
23. Colombia
24. 1986 World Cup
25. Mia Hamm, Michelle Akers
26. Six (6-1)
27. Rivaldo
28. Austria
29. Kim Milton Neilsen
30. USA and Switzerland

31. France and Mexico
32. France and West Germany
33. Egypt (26 goals)
34. Norway
35. Sweden
36. Brazil, Portugal and Angola
37. 1930

38. Hamburger SV (Hamburg)
39. David Platt
40. Six

41. Sixteen
42. Ferenc Puskas
43. Daniel Passarella
44. Pauleta (11 goals)
45. Peru
46. Sixteen
47. Ian Callaghan
48. Angola (ranked 60th)
49. Trinidad & Tobago
50. Brazil, Italy, Germany, Mexico

Quiz 2

1. Martin Keown
2. Jim Leighton
3. Ukraine, Serbia & Montenegro
4. Diana Ross
5. Ronaldo (ten goals)
6. Italy
7. Pickles
8. Japan
9. Uruguay, Argentina
10. Ali Daei

11. Thirteen
12. United Arab Emirates
13. Michelle Akers, Carin Jennings, April Heinrichs
14. Archie Thompson
15. Hassan (Hossam and Ibrahim)
16. Ken Aston
17. Czech Republic (ranked fourth in the world)
18. Turkey

19. Azerbaijan
20. Nine

21. Laszlo Kiss
22. Uruguay
23. England
24. Robert Prosinecki
25. April Heinrichs
26. Berne (Switzerland) 1954
27. Antonio Carbajal
28. Carolina Morace
29. Trinidad & Tobago
30. Landon Donovan

31. Spain, Switzerland, Slovakia
32. Laszlo Kiss
33. Ecuador
34. Paul Ince, Darren Anderton and Paul Scholes
35. Angola
36. Peru
37. Fifteen
38. Gary Neville
39. David McCreery
40. Cesare Maldini

41. Emile Heskey
42. Stefan Effenberg
43. 1994 World Cup
44. 46 years old
45. Three
46. Wolfgang Overath, Franz Beckenbauer
47. Jean Langenus
48. Ecuador
49. Mexico
50. Spain

**Look out for the other
brilliant quiz books
in this series.**

So You Think You Know
Premier League Football?
ISBN 0340 88190 9

So You Think You Know Test Cricket?
ISBN 0340 90293 0

So You Think You Know The Simpsons?
ISBN 0340 91715 6

So You Think You Know Doctor Who?
ISBN 0340 89422 9

So You Think You Know
The Lord of the Rings?
ISBN 0340 87361 2

Price £4.99

Available from good bookshops or from our
website, www.madaboutbooks.com